Printed in the United States of America.
First Printing, 2020

Publisher
Williams Commerce, LLC
Visit Our Website
Williamscommerce1.com
ISBN: 978-0-578-80879-6

Acknowledgements

Before opening up about my story, I would like to thank God for blessing me with this opportunity and platform to share my testimony. I desire to inspire the world one day at a time. From the bottom of my heart, I would like to thank those who helped me along the way that weren't mentioned in my book. Please don't think that I forgot about you. It's always the little things that make the biggest differences. With God's grace and mercy, I was able to turn the unthinkable into something legendary. This book wouldn't have come true without the amazing help of God, Michele A. Roberts, Sasha Austrie, Ross Williams, Williams Commerce Publishing Company, and everyone that contributed to my journey along the way.

Table of Contents

Chapter 1: The Unthinkable

Most childhood circumstances are deemed normal due to the surroundings being the first experience of a new life. Growing up in the Iberville Projects in New Orleans, Louisiana, never granted me a sense of normalcy. My humble beginnings began in a three-bedroom apartment that housed ten people. It would be fair to say that my competitive spirit was sparked from having to fight for scraps of less than adequately sized meals to feed the entire household and space to lie down on shared mattresses. My mother, two uncles, and an aunt headed the household with a host of my cousins. Stepping across the threshold of my project unit applied even more tension and pressure.

Occasionally, gunshots rang out in the night air or broad daylight only yards away from where I laid my head every night. My neighborhood, the 4th Ward, is notoriously known as one of the toughest neighborhoods in a city that is commonly referred to as the murder capital. Not only did I face the rigors of living in the housing projects, but I also had to face the sight of a cemetery every time I stepped onto my porch.

OG's and old heads with brown bags of liquor, the same stories, and no ambitions, crowded the surrounding porches of my unit. Drug dealers prowled the neighborhood along with their customers. My beautiful distraction from an ugly situation was the game that made me believe in love at first sight.

I first put on a football helmet and pads at five years old. The first positions I played were linebacker and running back. Early childhood affirmations from coaches and other players about my skills motivated me to draw that same appraisal from anyone who watched me play football.

Have you ever wanted something so bad that it felt like a living and breathing thing? It's something that rarely leaves your mind, is in sync with your spirit, and there is no separation from it. Football has always served as my something, plus more. It held my undivided attention for so long that I was not sure who I was without it.

I'd be making something up if I said I could pinpoint a specific person that influenced my initial interest in the sport. Football was what the streets and my neighborhood gave the kids to keep us out of trouble. Thankfully, I took the bait instead of being led astray down a destructive path that was easily susceptible and commonly traveled in the inner city. Most of my early grade school evenings after school were spent on the football field at Harrell Park in Uptown, New Orleans, and Goretti Saints Field in New Orleans East. That's where I learned the fundamentals of the game.

After delivering my first hit on the field, I identified an appropriate place to release the painful frustrations that fueled my real life. It gave me the escape I needed since I never got a chance to experience a vacation during my childhood. In the atmosphere of the New Orleans public school system, it felt as if those such as myself from the concrete jungle, who were forced to fight over food and endured harsh everyday struggles of the ghetto, were forgotten about. My smile remained throughout the tribulations, and it was a signal of relief and hope for the young boy in the mirror and others around me. I maintained my positive energy and stamina on and off the football field.

During my inaugural years on this earth, I subconsciously felt unprotected and was forced to grow up quickly. None of the four adults in the household could find or afford a way to prevent my siblings from living from pillar to post and in and out of other people's apartments. One of the best things about adversity is acquiring the ability to discover joy in the darkness.

In the middle of all this disarray, we still experienced good times mixed with family shenanigans. Horsing around and priceless laughs within that project unit were some of the fondest memories of my early childhood. The opposite types of memories were in abundance. The desire to have a close relationship with my mother appeared to be a never-ending chase during my early years. Maybe her emotions were lost in the middle of her chaotic life, or it could have been her drinking and gambling issues.

One memory is forever painted on my psyche, like a mural in the ghetto memorializing a beloved fallen soldier. That Tuesday night resembled a typical one in the Iberville Projects. You could hear chatter from those who hugged the porch from sunup to sundown, coupled with litter blowing over the unkept landscape of the project court. As usual, my mother was out and about probably at Harrah's Casino or gambling at a card game in the neighborhood. The regularity of the night stopped there.

My dad did not reside at the household in the 4th Ward, but he made his presence felt since the beginning of time. Usually, my mother acknowledged me when she returned home. However, this time when she returned home, she ignored me as my father frantically followed her upstairs with fire in his eyes.

Moments later, rumbling became evident. However, no one else downstairs acknowledged it. The innocence of my childhood was snatched when the sounds of my father's forceful hands caused my mother to gasp yells that still replay in my mind over twenty years later. While she pleaded for him to stop, I was the only one brave enough to try helping her.

I'd trade it all to erase the sight of what I saw when I made it upstairs. My father stood over my mother, unleashing violent punches. My heart crumbled while I watched the woman who gave me life receive a merciless beating. Although she had little regard for her baby boy, she was the helpless woman my dad frequently abused. My desperate cries for him to stop only caused a brief pause, which he used to tell me, "Get the fuck out of here!"

Regardless of all the additional commotion, nobody moved from their statuesque position downstairs. Although the beating soon subsided, it continued in my head. My father's frequent aggression appeared to manifest towards my mother, and no one else at the time. I always wondered, why? Is this normal? Did she do something to get beat? I still don't know the answers to those questions, but it's unjustifiable and those occurrences permanently stained my memory.

Soon my father, Bruce, would define these actions as "tough love." I calculated it as selfishness and abuse. It seemed as if no one ever taught him how to express his frustration other than with his fists and verbal tirades. Early in life, I learned to be intentional with what you ask for. I desired change and received it. One evening as the sun dropped into the evening sky, we returned home to all of our possessions outside. My mother usually shouldered rent, but it fell by her waist side. We'd been evicted.

This was the only thing that could break up what was headed nowhere fast. All of my siblings went into foster care, aside from my brother Henry and I, who is one year older than me. From what we knew at the time, we were our father's only biological children. After experiencing eviction, the ride away from the Iberville Projects closed a cold chapter in my life and opened a new one.

Chapter 2: "They" Called Him Boujee

I walked into uncertainty, but I felt as if I embarked upon a steppingstone of my destiny. While living in the Iberville Projects, I perceived my dad's situation different from reality. It seemed as if he left us to fend for ourselves in the inner-city while he enjoyed the outskirts. That was only partially true. His life was unstable at the time also, but what set him apart was his desire to never be complacent.

We bounced around a few places throughout the Big Easy and ended up settling at a place on Loyola Avenue when I was seven years old. Thankfully, we weren't bound to the projects anymore.

This fresh start let me know that there was another way to live other than the project lifestyle. On the exterior, it is easy to judge the man who brought me into this world, but there were other elements aside from his dark side. Single-parent households are typically headed by mothers. My father shouldered the responsibility of putting a roof over our heads, food on our tables, and clothes on our backs. Also, he passionately encouraged my involvement in football.

He viewed it as a way out of the life I endured. Football was supposed to be the rising tide that would lift my family's figurative ship out of a life of uncertainty, poverty, and chaos.

My father was firm in his beliefs. School and football were priorities, and everything else was background noise. This is not an indictment of a parent's single-mindedness. It is recognition of his principles. He believed in Henry and I enough to devote his time, effort, and "tough love." He lived vicariously through his sons and pushed his dream with so much force that it became mine.

Henry and I instantly put more on my father's plate than what he was accustomed to. That didn't slow him down though. If anything, it upped his grind. We knew about our father's work ethic before moving in with him. Many other adults were entertained by his hustling ways and earned reputation. In the true sense of the word, my father was a hustler. He did whatever necessary to feed his family. We had a perception about how he lived, and now we would witness it for ourselves as he forged a life for his growing family.

My mother, Liz Theophile, was the apple of my dad's eyes. A blind man with his back turned could vividly see her beauty. She didn't understand her worth. My dad desired to elevate my mom from her lifestyle, but the Theophile family considered him boujee. It would take serious adaptation to adjust her mind and way of living from the only way she ever knew. My father couldn't settle for that type of life. As rough as he treated her, he could not turn her around. After having four kids, two of whom he fathered, bad habits, chronic poverty, and frequent beatings by my father, nothing motivated her to change. My mom was committed to the way she conducted her life without my dad's idea of intervention.

My father's insecurities surfaced. He experienced a hard time coming to grips that she wouldn't change, even for him. My dad thought his words were law and gold. "You better do what I say," was his mentality. He gave my mother a few kids, but he never put a ring on it. Not doing so isn't a rare occurrence, but he still wanted her to do better and tried to get her to do so through submission.

My dreams and visions were vivid during my grade school years. All I wanted was a family like the perfect ones I saw on television, such as The Cosby's or Family Matters. While living with my mother, I kept to myself and away from all the bickering that a crowded apartment maintained. It would have been much different had my mother allowed my father to lead, but my father's ways didn't leave her much optimism. His ways gave me an understanding of her stance. If he attempted to sell my mother on the thought that his way was better by way of his fists, I could see why she said no. My family becoming the Cosby's was out of sight and out of mind.

When I was six years old, my father gave me a light fade I'd never forget. Halfway through cutting my hair, he put the clippers down and said, "Listen, I'm changing your name. It is not Devin anymore, and your last name is no longer Theophile. When you go to Thomalaphone Elementary school, your name is now Delvin. I added an "L" in your first name, and your last name is now the same as mine, Breaux."

After an awkward silence, I responded, "My name is Devin. What are you talking about?" He immediately barked back, "What the hell did I just tell you?" For the first six years of my life, my name was Devin Theophile. The name my aunt selected for me instantly became part of the past, and my father officially renamed me Delvin Breaux.

In my heart, I am still a Theophile, but legally I am Delvin Breaux. My name change made me curious about my mother's family history. Our roots were four generations deep in New Orleans before my arrival. My great-great grandfather was the first black Bank Teller, at Whitney Bank in the city. Still, on my mother's side, there is a big contingent of Jefferson's from Vacherie, Louisiana. I always imagined that researching my family heritage might lead me to my forty acres and a mule.

Our creamy beige shotgun house on Loyola Avenue, with two bathrooms and bedrooms was next door to my grandmother's house. My paternal grandfather turned his back on my father before he was born. They went without meeting until my father was in high school.

During that one opportunity, my grandfather shoo'd him away to continue watching Soul Train. Regardless of my father's unfavorable actions and treatment, he broke a generational curse, and I am proud of him for that.

Henry and I did our thing on the football field, and my father loved it to the fullest. Quickly into our park ball days, it became evident that Henry was the golden child. We both received attention, but he got the better of it. My dad often demanded me to do things the way my brother did them. A new trend in my childhood emerged once I began receiving whippings for not keeping up with Henry on the track after football practice. My dad always wanted me to be in the front with Henry, but no one could keep up with him, including myself.

When practices finished, I could see the disgust on his face, and he continuously threatened me by saying, "The next time you are not in the front with Henry, I'm going to bust your ass!" I wondered, "Why was that worth an ass whipping?" I assumed I'd get a little more attention and love if I obeyed his command. After most practices, my father's demonic stare resembled the same look I saw in his eyes as a four-year old kid while he beat my mother.

My father's force and my God-given gifts made me a standout on the football field as soon as I stepped on it. I channeled all of my energy derived from my family's emotional and physical dysfunction onto the field. The teams I played for were built around what I could do on the gridiron.

Carrying teams to several championships became a gratifying and reoccurring experience. I played for the Harrell Rams from 1994 - 96 and then played for the Goretti Saints in New Orleans East.

I didn't immediately grasp that I was no longer Devin Theophile. People around me mirrored my confusion. Friends, family, and peers still occasionally referred to me as Devin. Periodically, I'd still write Devin Theophile on top of my school papers. While the transition lingered, I realized that this was a problem that needed to be tackled head on.

During one of my most important football games with Goretti, I grew the urge to put a stamp on my new name. The typical standout plays such as solo tackles, sacks, or forcefully shedding blocks weren't the statements I envisioned because I already made them. As the first quarter ended, I smelled blood from the opposing team.

They maintained a similar record as us, but I felt they weren't on the same level as my team. During the beginning of the second quarter I noticed the interior linemen had a hard time blocking me when I blitzed from the linebacker position.

I hadn't conjured up a thought about what statement I'd make until the ball was snapped on a third down moments before halftime. While the center and left guard approached the line out of the huddle, they looked so winded that I knew they wouldn't rise up quickly to block me after the ball was snapped.

Before the high-pitched quarterback yelled, "Hut!", I was already in full throttle as a cheetah a few strides away from his prey in the open jungle. Once the quarterback extended the ball to hand it off to his running back, I snatched it and jetted in the opposite direction. My momentum and everyone's shock resulted in me winding up in the other team's endzone before everyone realized what happened. Anyone who was on the field that night, would never forget the name Delvin Breaux.

I accomplished my mission and it was evident my father held my skills and potential in higher regard after that game. Before that night, I felt like he only believed in Henry, but he became verbal about his belief in me going forward. I knew I was a reflection of his aggression on the football field. He started verbalizing what he always saw. His words now reflected his thoughts, and he would say, "I know you have something special."

Chapter 3: My Guardian Angel

When my brother and I stepped on the field, we became known as the Breaux Brothers. They called my brother Butter and me Chocolate Chip. The Breaux Brothers were known on every football field in the area, and we could not be stopped. My dad proudly bragged, "My boy can play!" whenever he referred to me. Some of my favorite childhood memories consisted of my dad cheering me along on the sidelines. When I made a great play, he would make eye contact with me and pump his balled fist, then cheeringly yell, "Yes sir! Good job, baby!" I often wondered where that brightness was suppressed during his dark moments when I made mistakes.

All of my life I heard various stories about whether my dad was a next-level football player or not. I know he played high school ball, but after that, the story gets kind of blurry. One time I heard that he was given a chance to workout with the Washington Redskins, but it never materialized because his first serious girlfriend was pregnant with my oldest sister, April. According to him, his family curtailed his opportunity to play professionally.

Years later, he decided to "rescue" my brother Henry and I from the Iberville Projects after he and my mom decided that living with him was best for us. My mother said she did what she had to do at the time because there was no telling how Henry and I would have turned out remaining in the projects. The surrounding violence and chaos could have led us down a different path more commonly traveled for those growing up in such hectic environments. I am forever thankful for her decision because it molded me into the king I am today.

My dad's stories from his past intrigued me. Both of my parents ran track and were stellar athletes at George Washington Carver High School in the 9th Ward of New Orleans. He also played football in high school, and some aspects of his childhood were more challenging than mine. My dad didn't know his father, and my grandmother raised him by herself. She was a devout Jehovah's Witness. Not only did she not celebrate holidays, but she also did not believe in sports either. It was fair to assume her beliefs put a damper on my father's football career. According to him, he was good enough to play at a local university, and then transfer to LSU. His inability to follow through with his dreams may be why he pushed my brother and I to continue playing. He lived vicariously through us. His passion for football was one of the reasons I hung onto the dream of making it big. I have not dug into any archives at George Washington Carver High School or LSU, and I refuse to. Why should I take away from his fond memories about his playing days, whether they are fabricated or not? Those recollections deeply inspired me and still do.

My stepmom was also heavily involved in supporting my brother and I. She loved us just like she gave birth to us. Although my dad never put a ring on her finger either, she was there for my brother and I. When we moved in with my dad, she already knew us. While we lived in the Iberville Projects, she periodically babysat us when we visited our dad. Saying nice things about her now is a far cry from my thoughts when I was much younger.

When she first came into my life, I didn't have much of an opinion of her. Once she transitioned from occasionally visiting to living with us in New Orleans

East, my feelings towards her soured. I wanted my real mom and my dad to be together and have a perfect little family. Her taking my mom's place did not sit well with me. I visualized that my mother would come to our little shotgun house with her bags, and we would live happily ever after. I gave Virginia hell, plus I was disrespectful and nearly belligerent to her. When she moved in it destroyed any hopes of having what I dreamed of seeing on television. It pained me that Virginia, and not my biological mother, was going to play Mrs. Huxtable.

As time went by, I saw how real Virginia was. One evening shortly after my family dynamic was altered, my dad blew my mind for the millionth time. As we exited the interstate on Chef Highway in New Orleans East, my dad demanded that we call Virginia mom. I appreciated her for not requiring us to do so. It was as if she knew what to do to make me love her. Virginia was not trying to replace my mom. She just embraced her place in our lives and played her role well. I could not help but accept it.

Virginia filled the roles of my mom and go-to person. Adjusting took some time and was no easy task. How do you tell a six-year old that his birth mother is out of the picture and your former babysitter is taking over her place? I don't know of one child who handled their birthparent's separation easily. Although my parents never lived together, I always hoped they eventually would. This setup ruined my hopes. Sure, there are tons of people who never lived with both of their biological parents under the same roof and many more who never knew their father. However, my situation was different. My father was there, and my "stepmom" became my guardian angel.

Our household was religion-less. Besides the interjection of my paternal grandmother being a Jehovah's Witness, there was no practice of faith. We had faith in our abilities, but a religious faith was not a part of my upbringing. Moving from the projects provided a new sense of stability. At this point, I already experienced a lot of hardships. Fighting over food, seeing a graveyard every day at my old place, circumstances of a broken home, and living in a public housing development caused me to form a rough exterior. More than likely, that's why I gave Virginia such a hard time. I had a survivor's mentality, and I did not want her to think I needed her. But here I am, living with my dad, my stepmom, Henry, Janae, my sister, and Derek, my younger brother. Our family grew over the years. Towards the end of my elementary school years, I experienced enough growth to apologize for the hell I gave her and expressed my love for her.

Virginia protected my siblings and I from our dad. I am forever grateful that she was there. Sometimes it is hard for me to fathom that I had such adult thoughts and experiences while I was so young. Many will probably not understand how much I went through before I turned six. Several years between the time of Virginia moving in until I left home at eighteen are somewhat blurry. I remember things like they are excerpts out of a book. There were some bumpy patches, but Virginia constantly supported me every step of the way and helped lay the foundation for my future.

Virginia's support wasn't the only thing constant throughout my upbringing. My dad continually struggled with relationships. It was evident by how he treated my mother Liz and stepmom Virginia. Although I had to deal with much of his abusive ways while my brother and I lived with him, it would have been much worse if Virginia was not there. She did her best to intervene when my dad's anger boiled over, and he wanted to unjustly punish me for minor infractions. She would talk him down, and I would escape momentarily. Most of the abuse she absorbed would have made its way to one of us if she were not there. My dad's emotional issues were deeper than any of our behavioral infractions. Sometimes I felt that Virginia stayed in the relationship to protect us from my dad's rage.

Chapter 4: Size 10

A picture must be painted of the abuse I experienced to be transparent about what I overcame, provide healing for those abused, and bring awareness to abusers. I still do not believe my father fully comprehends what he put us through. You hear about children being abused, and on occasion, you hear the story relayed from their own mouths. Switches, rulers, and belts cannot be considered the only way to enforce discipline on young children. This is my first time disclosing these details.

Under the care of my dad, my childhood cannot be compared to anything other than torture. I didn't know what it felt like to live without getting ass whippings. Covering receivers and stopping the run were plays I always knew how to make, but blocking painful thoughts out of my mind didn't come so easily. Haunted nights became a regularity. There was no coaching available to train me on how to defend myself against harsh memories. My aggressiveness on the field was my superpower, but it couldn't combat all of my problems. Emotional torture cannot be tackled, but it must be stopped. I am still in need of rescue and healing from the bruises of my childhood, even now as an adult. Giving up was never an option. Not then, not now, not ever. I vividly recall not being able to shower or sit down due to the beatings I received. As no child, I was not perfect, but no one deserves what I received.

One of the worst beatdowns I received was with a Louisville Slugger baseball bat at the age of eleven. I can still hear my cries for dear life that I yelled out as he beat on me like I was a pinata at a kindergartner's birthday party. Everyone was home as my dad thought he was Barry Bonds, and I was a baseball coming across the middle of the plate. No one who resided there wore a hearing aid or had hearing problems. These were not the typical cries from an average whipping for disobeying the rules. I was beaten across my back, on my arms, ass, and legs because I couldn't recite all of the states in the U.S. The pain of no one coming to save me that day still lingers as I write this.

My deepest thoughts wouldn't allow me to understand why no one stepped up for me while getting beat and tortured. But then again, I was the only one at four years old who intervened when my mother got beat to her lowest. I was the youngest, but the bravest. Others were more scared of him and knew they'd get what I received if they tried stopping him. I knew my mom's siblings and other people heard my father beating my biological mother in the Iberville Projects. Plus, I knew my cries didn't go unheard. I hopelessly hoped that my cries of anguish would somehow pierce my dad's mind to let him know I could not take anymore. Consequently, my household in the East turned me into the Incredible Hulk.

Things came to a head when I was around the age of nine when I had some rare alone time after being violently punished for minor misbehavior. The reoccurring punishment on the menu that week was to kneel on uncooked rice on an old white tile floor in the kitchen for an hour or two depending on how he was feeling. While watching the other kids play, and sharp edges from uncooked rice penetrated my kneecaps, I concocted an idea to deal with the abuse.

Towards the end of the week, when everyone left the house while I was punished, I scurried to search for one of my dad's private possessions. Once I got to the top of the closet, I retrieved his gun. That motherfucker was heavy. As soon as I felt the weight of the gun, my father turned into the driveway. My 40 yard dash times don't compare to the speed I used putting the gun back and returning to the rice. The suicidal thoughts subsided while I retreated to the spot where I knelt in the dark. Enduring what I was told to do took the place of ending it all that night.

I could not understand why all of this was happening to me. Another visualization of my past that remains in my mind is when I yelled at my reflection in the mirror with a face filled with tears screaming, "I'm nothing! Why is this happening to me?" Here I am going to school and practice every day, trying my best to excel and be a blessing to others, but was still subject to continuous torture behind closed doors.

The beatings elevated with age. Henry and I attended Francis W. Gregory for junior high. One day during our 6th grade math class I wrote down our homework problems, but Henry forgot to do the same. Before starting my homework that evening I shared the questions with him. Shortly after that, my father viciously tore into me with the Size 10. I rarely understood why I received whippings and just felt that my father hated me. He progressively found new ways to ensure the beatings hurt worse. The bat was only one tool of his torture. My dad was so passionate about disciplining us that he created something new to beat us with. The Size 10 was designed with his steel toe work boots that he wrapped with tape and swung with all of his might.

Another clear memory of being terrorized occurred during the eighth grade. During class, my friend John tapped me on the shoulder to ask a question. As soon as I turned my head to answer him, the teacher caught me and uttered the words I could not bear to hear, "I'm going to call your dad!" Why couldn't she just give me some extra work? Instead, she told this terrified thirteen-year old boy that she was going to tell his dad. My teacher probably assumed, "He must come from a pretty good home to have his dad involved in his life, and a little male enforcement would keep me straight in her class." If only she knew the terror she inflicted on my young mind for the rest of the school day. It was like waiting for three o'clock to fight the three hundred pound school bully.

The weather after school that day matched my mood. I refused to go straight home on that dark and rainy afternoon. I took a different route towards my grandmother's house on Warrington Drive and ran like a wild child looking for safety. All I could hope to do was prolong the inevitable. Once I arrived at her door, my legs began trembling like the leg on a collapsing table, then I began knocking. While pounding against her door, my fear boiled over, and I went to the bathroom on myself. My tears were flowing faster than the windy raindrops that lightly flooded the street when my grandmother opened the door. Once I entered, I voiced my fear that my dad would kill me when he got home, and she asked, "Are you scared? You're shaking!" Although she was staring at me, she couldn't comprehend the severity of my state of mind. Some of my father's actions were learned behaviors from her.

My grandmother was a single mother who used ass whippings to keep her son in line and discipline him. Both of them called their brutal form of punishment "tough love." Neither one could see their faults and felt it was plausible. My grandmother must have called him at her earliest convenience because my dad appeared shortly after I arrived to take me home. My punishment was to hold encyclopedias. If one dropped, I got busted on my ass with the Size 10. I never confused the torture for "tough love." There was nowhere to turn or hide from the abuse, but I knew I had to make it come to an end.

Chapter 5: The Last Beat Down

Regardless of all I went through, I was still very popular in school and had great relationships with others. It was challenging having to hide the trauma I went through at home. Most people in the neighborhood and surrounding areas knew about the Breaux Boys. Not only were we standouts on the field, but we were also taught to respect those in authority and how to treat others. That was strange coming from a household where the dad disregarded how his children felt. However, my stepmom's interjections provided a slight sense of balance. We said, "Yes ma'am" or "No ma'am" when addressing our elders. We did not talk back nor give our coaches or teachers a hard time. I may have been the last person that people expected to receive such abuse behind closed doors.

One day while I tried venting to my cousin, he responded, "Lil nigga! You are Michael Jackson, and he is Joe Jackson!" I agreed with the analogy and blindly used it as justification for my beatings. I knew my father wanted me to be great, and I knew Michael Jackson experienced child abuse as well. It was as if the world gave Michael Jackson the love his father was supposed to show him. Becoming excellent at my craft seemed like the blueprint to obtain the love I desired. Ironically, my cousin was pretty perceptive. I may not be as soft-spoken as Michael, but his childhood appeared similar to what I endured.

The most horrendous beat down took place over a bag of corn chips in the variety pack of chips which consisted of Cheetos, Cool Ranch and Nacho Doritos, Plain Lays, and those original fucking Corn Chips. My stepmom and younger sister Janae were out of town at her AAU competition. That evening my little brother Derek and I were returning from our grandmother's house, while Henry visited our aunt. My father was cutting my hair in the bathroom while we waited on Henry's arrival. As soon as my brother arrived, my dad cut off the clippers and called for Derek, Henry, and I to come into the kitchen.

While we stood dumbfounded, our dad asked us, "Who ate the last bag of corn chips?" Neither one of us liked corn chips, so we knew it was someone else as soon as we looked at each other. We all denied eating them, even after his rage escalated. Once my dad had enough, he furiously made us open our mouths, so he could check for corn chip residue. To no surprise, none of us showed any signs of eating them, and we still got our ass busted. He decided that a beat down would bring out a confession of who ate the chips.

We were all told to strip and prepare for the "normal" punishment, so we all bent over on the living room couch butt naked. I stood in the middle of my brothers, and our dad began beating us with the Size 10. We continued denying it, and then he began punching Henry. As no one was confessing to eating the nasty ass chips, our dad started stomping Henry then put his knee on his neck. Derek quickly and falsely admitted to eating the chips. My dad turned to relieve his rage on Derek, and I said, "Yup, he ate them!" so we could stop getting abused. Then he stared into my soul with the same demonic look in his eyes from when I was four years old and yelled, "Shut the fuck up! No one was talking to you!"

Those words momentarily distracted our dad. Then he left out of the room to find something else to whip us with. As he hurried in search of something to inflict more pain on us, Henry said, "Fuck this shit, I'm running away y'all!" Then he bolted through the door faster than I ever saw him run. He made it out wearing only gym shorts and a t-shirt. My dad stormed out of the back door as Derek and I watched his steps. This discipline was headed to the next level if that was possible. We were living in a horror movie. The pitch-black stormy night set the tone for my father's rage.

My dad retrieved a tire iron that you jack your car up with from the garage. Derek and I huddled together in a corner, petrified that this would be our last day on earth. When my dad returned and realized Henry left, he stopped beating us to search for him. Henry's escape saved our lives. What was my dad planning to do with a tire iron over the bodies of three of his children being punished for his belief that they ate a bag of fucking corn chips?

I found out the next day where Henry ran off to. He ran for dear life and pleaded with anyone that would help him. A stranger in the community heard the anguish in his voice about what took place and brought him to the police station.

Henry is light-skinned, so his bruising was apparent, but he still had to plead his case when he got to the police station. His first encounter was with a white police officer who believed Henry and allowed him to tell the whole story. However, a black officer overheard the commotion and intervened.

Shortly after my dad arrived, the black officer sided with him and justified physical whippings on teenage boys who are misbehaving. I cannot imagine how my brother felt on that silent ride home from the police station. Later I understood that he believed Henry's reason for running was evidence of his guilt. I am not sure what clicked in my dad's head after this incident. When my stepmom finally returned home from the AAU trip with Janae, she came into the bathroom and saw how badly we were abused. My brothers and I had whelps, scratches, bruised legs and backs, and our asses looked like they were bleeding. We cried and collectively thanked God for her return. Tears filled her eyes once she saw our conditions.

The next day, he suggested that we were getting too big for "whippings," and he would start talking to us more to help him gain some understanding. Maybe he was snatched into reality once he conceptualized that if Henry had just pulled down his shorts, he would probably still be in jail today. The black officer unknowingly saved him from what would have certainly been charges of child abuse. My dad most likely realized this as soon as he entered the police station. This same thought probably stuck with him on the ride home. I can see why he said nothing. His thoughts were most likely haunting him.

Chapter 6: The Breaux Show

The biggest shift that occurred throughout my middle school years was developing a career mindset. Some of the peers I grew up with that were freshman already started carving out a name for themselves on the varsity scene at their respective high schools. My middle school, which is better known around the New Orleans area as Gregory, stopped at 9th grade. Therefore, we weren't classified to play anything higher than Junior Varsity. In retrospect, I didn't conceptualize the opportunity of playing varsity as a freshman. Being loyal to the moment and circumstance made me get the most out of my current situation. Playing at Gregory held my undivided attention while I enjoyed my final year of middle school, but which high school I would attend lurked in the back of my mind.

The catholic league in New Orleans, which consists of several all-boys catholic high schools throughout the metropolitan area, developed a reputation for giving athletes the best chance to play at the next level. Being one of the city's best players, that's where I expected to go. Jesuit and Holy Cross were the first two schools to capture my attention.

New Orleans schools consisted of an upspoken dynamic during my era of grade school. The majority of the schools were either all-white or all-black, and very few in-between existed. As with inequality, the all-black schools possessed lesser of the resources, which equates to fewer opportunities. I was simply impressed that Jesuit served hot wings for school lunch when I visited.

While walking through those unfamiliar hallways, I realized that I was more than just sheltered socially. I'd been sheltered culturally as well. Seeing Asian, White, Black, Spanish, and other ethnicities learn in the same classroom gave me a glance at how the real world functions. At my previous schools, the only people that weren't black were in leadership positions on campus. Many nuances of social engineering don't show themselves until decades after the programming.

Go with the flow didn't become a cool term until I was in my twenties. My father gave us no choice but to go with his flow. I voiced and internalized where I wanted to go for high school, but he was the shot caller or, for lack of a better term, dictator.

Louisiana has always ranked amongst the top states for producing professional athletes and top-ranked college players. The New Orleans public school system has consistently stood as a big contributor to that. Most of the New Orleans public high schools lacked the culture, longevity, and resources as the catholic schools, but it was a well-traveled route.

Not only was it a well-traveled route, but it was a route that I'd be traveling on because my father shut down my catholic school aspirations. All of my father's football-related decisions paid off, including Goretti, Gregory, and his training methods. Where he enrolled us for high school appeared to keep his streak of great football choices consecutive. Most schools promised me a starting position, but the Head Coach at my new school let me know that everything on his team had to be earned. I wouldn't have wanted it any other way, and that made me aware of our matching values.

I quickly took heed that performing at a high level gained the respect of others, and I wanted all of mine. Going the extra mile was the only route I ever knew. Most of that extra mile during my sophomore year was spent in the weight room getting my body adjusted to playing at a higher level. While racking the weights one particular evening after a workout when most people vacated the building, I grew weary of an inevitable occurrence and situation I never thought I'd experience.

My father worked at my high school as a track coach. Although he hadn't laid hands on me since the night Henry went to the police station, I didn't know what he was capable of and wasn't thrilled to find out either. Sometimes I wondered if he would try to assert his dominance of me in front of others at our school. The interaction was unavoidable, but hadn't occurred yet, so I remained on my toes when I knew he could potentially be around.

On this day, I had a minor run-in with a math teacher, so I was on guard while wrapping up a workout in the weight room. I heard a noise in the gym while exiting the weight room that I assumed was my father. I thought about not even checking to see if it was him before going the other way, but something told me to check anyway.

To my surprise, my father was nowhere in sight. The Head Coach of the football team, who was a father figure to many on and off the field, was sweeping the gym floor. I didn't need to see his job description to know that sweeping wasn't part of his assignments. Even if we would have used the gym floor to practice, I couldn't imagine him doing that before seeing him in action that evening. Maybe it was because I never saw a Head Coach perform that type of task, but Coach Wayne Reese was different.

Proudly performing behind the scenes was a common task of his. Many other times, such as that one, I'd see him from a distance cleaning the gym floor, parking lot, weight room, or locker room, and didn't say anything. I guess God gave us two eyes and one mouth, so we could observe twice as much as we speak. Watching how Coach Reese functioned incorporated new aspects into my DNA.

I appeared on my dream college's radar before my first varsity game when I caught the attention of an LSU scout during a summer camp going into my sophomore season. During that interaction, I hadn't officially secured the starting spot on paper, but the scout's assuredness solidified my status mentally. The opposing starting cornerback on my team was already getting recruited, and that served as an opportunity to perform in front of pre-existing eyes and attract new ones.

My plans went accordingly, and I secured the starting position. Throughout the season, I began growing antsy because I wanted to make more plays, but quarterbacks began avoiding throwing in my direction. When we played St. Augustine, my tenth-grade year seemed like the opportunity to do so. They were the only black all boys school in the catholic league and produced many NFL athletes such as Tyrann Mathieu, Leonard Fournette, plus a host of others.

The Friday night lights felt as if they were directly on the field that night. The crowd did also. It became the most packed game I ever played in before everyone piled into the sold-out stadium.

The game came down to the last possession. We were up 12-7. All they needed was one touchdown to potentially put a lingering L in our legacy. The proverbial island that a cornerback is on had a spotlight on it. I knew they might mix in a running play or two at the most because time was running out, and they were more than seventy yards away from scoring. If they accomplished that, the secondary would be looked at as the people who gave the game up. The quarterback had no choice but to look down the field, and I wanted him to never forget looking my way.

On the first snap, the quarterback dropped back. The receiver I lined up against, who was one of the fastest players in the city, ran full speed in my direction. I didn't jump his route to avoid guessing wrong and giving up a game-ending touchdown. I saw the hitch coming and covered it. The quarterback never laid eyes on it and threw an incomplete pass in the other direction.

The time stopped after the incomplete pass, so I figured this was their opportunity to call their run play. My football IQ paid off two plays in a row. A play on third down in the opposite direction ignited my sense of urgency to make a play. Each second of this drive replays in my mind vividly because I gave it my undivided attention.

The stadium contained thousands of people eyeing the football field illuminated by the Tad Gormley lights. They shined their brightest on 4th down when the receiver started the snap mirroring his movements on first down. Once the ball snapped into the quarterback's hands, my name was written on it. Seconds later, I knew where the ball was headed, then jumped the hitch route and ended the game by batting the ball to the ground when it was thrown in my direction.

I could hear the stadium and my teammates erupt after I made the game-deciding play. Henry was one of the first people I spotted in the madness. We immediately ran to each other and celebrated. That joint moment of excitement and accomplishment solidified that our game reached new heights. Also, that play made me view my moniker in a different light. The Breaux Show name was no longer a term I took lightly. That night I impacted more people than the ones in shoulder pads and headsets. Students and alumni had bragging rights, the news stations had positive news to report, and the fans got their money's worth. The impact I made that night dwarfed the ones I dreamed of then and eventually lived out, but the vision began unraveling. The only person on the field who knew what I fought through to get to that moment was Henry. My private battles and adversities weren't publicized at that stage, but it became a life purpose to let the world know what the Breaux Show stands for.

Chapter 7: Hurricane Katrina

My family and I, including Virginia, Janae, Derek, and my little brother Brandon left five days before Hurricane Katrina made landfall. My dad and Henry waited behind a couple of days to ride out the hurricane, but once they declared immediate evacuations, they left ASAP and went to Houston. Cars were already bumper to bumper on I-10 when we left several days early to evacuate to my Aunt Jimmy's house in Baton Rouge, Louisiana. The interstate consisted of an overflow of evacuees, cars blasting loud music, people yelling out of their vehicles at the top of their lungs, horns honking, and smells of foul manure.

We all had to share a room, which was something we were accustomed to doing. We planned on only staying there for a few days and returning home, but Hurricane Katrina tore into those plans and damaged the city I'd grown to love deeply. Mother nature presented another form of adversity into my trauma filled life. Our house was severely molded and held three feet of floodwater. My dad hired a team of contractors as soon as it was safe to start rebuilding.

I decided to remain with my step-mother because I felt safer with her than my dad, plus I loved being with her and my siblings. We developed an unbreakable bond. We eventually had to move out of Aunt Jimmy's house and find somewhere else to stay.

Our new home was in a nearby trailer park. It was cool, but I never thought I'd ever reside in a trailer or live outside of New Orleans before college. We lived in a spacious double-wide trailer with four bedrooms and two bathrooms. My siblings and I enrolled in Southern University Lab School on Southern University's campus. Our life changed in the blink of an eye. Soon, my dad and Henry joined us in Baton Rouge, and we reunited as a family again. This time it was much different because all the ass whippings were a part of the past. During this time period, my dad was a very calm person. He was still a no-nonsense type of guy, but with less aggression.

Thankfully, we were allowed to join the football team right away. The ease of the competition reminded me of my park ball days at Goretti. I started my first game only one week after enrolling. I had to settle in and accept the possibility that we may never go back home or see New Orleans again. Our first game was against Clinton High. They were a pretty decent football team. During the first half, I racked up three tackles, one sack, and one forced fumble. I played with my hair on fire, as my coach would say.

My first play of the second half was on the kick return team. I was lined up on the second row and not expecting the ball to come my way. Coincidentally, that's exactly what happened. The ball came straight to me.

Once I took off running with the football, a defender laid his helmet directly on my left Fibula-Tibia. I immediately grabbed my leg and started screaming. Shortly after being helped to the sidelines, I was diagnosed with a broken leg. Boom, there goes my full season. I had to watch my teammates ball out and come up short at reaching the state championship game. Watching and not being able to help devastated me because I knew I could have made a difference if I was healthy. We remained in Baton Rouge until April and returned home when our school, McDonogh 35 Senior High reopened.

Chapter 8: Broken

The summer of 2006 allowed Henry and I a much-needed break before deciding which college football scholarship we would accept. We are not twins, but we were in the same grade. Going on summer college tours with Henry and my father served as some of life's best memories. We finally received the respect we fought for our entire upbringing. Beatings from our father were a part of the past. I received over 30 Division I college scholarship offers. My brother and I were voted blue chip athletes and top recruits in the nation. During the summer of 2006, I made a verbal commitment to LSU, and my brother verbally committed to Ole Miss. We were finally living the life we dreamed of while playing pitch up tackle in the Iberville Projects and spending countless hours on the football field where we poured our blood, sweat, and tears.

Way before we started our playing days in high school, my dad made a conscientious decision. He wanted us to get the best opportunity to play football and be recognized for our skills. The goal was getting a college scholarship, then on to the NFL. Our high school was across town, but my dad saw the historic high school that graduated NFL Super Bowl Champion Neil Smith and NFL Reporter with ESPN Analyst Michael Smith, as the best opportunity to accomplish our educational and athletic goals.

We made it unscathed to our senior year. There was no going to parties, no cellphones, and definitely no girlfriends, before then. Now I could look forward to dating and going to the prom. My stepmom spoke up to my dad on our behalf. She told him to let us grow up and allow us to have cell phones and girlfriends. It was time for us to have our own thoughts and make good decisions. Who was going to think for us when we left for college? My dad was still countering and voicing his opinion about the downsides of having a girlfriend while in school. He said they'd be a distraction, slow us down, and make us unfocused. To me, it did not matter. There was some freedom on the horizon with a girlfriend, a cell phone, college in a year, and eventually the NFL.

I fell in love for the first time during my senior year with my best friend Jasmine. Even after we went our separate ways, she remained on my mind. Jasmine was the most gorgeous girl I'd ever seen. Also, she was the captain of the dance team and one of the most popular girls at school. Jasmine began bringing my lunch to school, so I returned the favor and matched her energy. My stepmom would say, that's so sweet of y'all. We used to make sandwiches and bring chips almost every day. Jasmine rarely ate school lunch because her parents made big money, and she didn't qualify for the free lunch our public school provided. It felt like we were on a picnic date every day when we ate our lunch in the courtyard in front of everyone. It was embarrassing at first, but she didn't care and was unapologetic about it, which made me love her even more. Jasmine gave me light in knowing I can love someone and showed me what reciprocal love was. I don't know what Jasmine is doing now, but if she reads this, and I hope she does, I want her to know I always cared about her and I always will and wish nothing but the best for her.

Now it was time to play ball. On the morning of one of our first games of the year, our dad woke us up blaring "Gangsta Party" by 2pac. The legendary 2pac track was our anthem on game days in the Breaux household for as long as I could remember. While my father was bringing us to morning practice, he received a call. He continued looking forward in silence for the next several blocks, and then he dryly said that he was just informed an LSU scout would be at the game. I knew he wouldn't have kept the same energy if Ole Miss was coming. He would hardly be able to contain himself. For whatever reason, he experienced a drawback showing me the same love he showed my siblings.

The energy in the car slightly shifted, but I broke the awkward silence by telling Henry, "You and some of the teammates have to rise to the occasion, so y'all can join me as an LSU Tiger." The facts that it was a beautiful day and only two days after my 17th birthday helped me carry on and enjoy the day leading up to the big game.

We were playing against Jesuit, one of our best non-conference opponents. We had not beaten a catholic school team in quite some time. There was a little extra motivation to make a good showing. Jesuit was a school I initially wanted to attend. I felt I had something to prove, and LSU scouts were going to be in the stands. I wanted them to know that it was no mistake choosing to recruit Delvin Breaux. They needed to know that no matter the score, I was always going to give it my all and leave everything on the field every time. This seventeen-year old senior was going to show them.

The game started off as I imagined. We were doing our thing and led 13-0 at halftime. During halftime, my coaches kept saying, "We need to make a play! Somebody has to make a play!" A fire ignited inside of me to be that person.

Our kickoff team was short a player to start the third quarter, so the Special Teams coach said, "Eh Breaux, we need you!" while I was preparing with the defense to take the field on the next play. I hadn't practiced with special teams all week, but I obliged. Aside from always following coaches' requests, I wanted to show the LSU scouts that I wasn't just a cornerback, and I could play special teams.

My best friend at the time, Frank, said, "I bet you aren't going to make this hit." I replied, "Bet." I was focused on keeping the other team's gain as little as possible. As the ball teed off, I ate up the yards as I sprinted down the field and thought I was Usain Bolt at the 20-yard line. Once I neared my target, I dove in headfirst, then the opposing player's knee caught my helmet, and jerked my neck back. I fell to the ground and instantly stopped moving, then everything went dark. The first words I heard were my teammates saying, "D Breaux get up! We need you! Let's go D Breaux!" My subconscious told me that I was good, but I couldn't move. Their requests faded out, then a bright white light appeared. It reminded me of the scene in Bruce Almighty when Morgan Freeman played God and brought Jim Carrey into an all-white room. It was unexplainable and otherworldly. I knew God and Heaven was calling my name, but it was not my time. Within a few seconds, my coach woke me up by placing smelling salt underneath my nose. My Head Coach, Wayne Reese's voice broke through the fog and asked, "You alright?" I mustered up the strength to say, "Yes. I'm good. I'm good."

I regained enough strength to walk off the field under my own power and take my helmet off. In high school, you must sit out a play or two if you get hurt. To stay loose and prepare to re-enter the game, I started jumping on the sideline. Suddenly, I felt a sharp pain shooting down my neck. Then I turned around and walked by my dad who was also on the sidelines. Once I told him that my neck was bothering me, he gave me a few Ibuprofens. The pills got stuck in my esophagus before they could enter my system. I later found out that my disk slipped into my esophagus. Coughing up the pills caused excruciating pain to shoot from my neck to my back. At that point, I knew it was not a twinge or a passing injury. No smelling salts or ibuprofen could stop this reality. I professed to my dad that, "Something is really bothering me," as I pointed to the back of my neck. Once I pointed, I roared out, "Get the ambulance! Get the ambulance now!" to my dad.

The ambulance quickly pulled over to where I was, and the paramedics came over to assess the situation. As I sat on the bench, they brought over a board to stabilize me. Then a brace was put on my neck, and I was strapped to the stretcher. While being rolled away, I heard a sound I often heard when it was time to come home, my stepmom's whistle. That was the family signal to come in for the evening. I did not see her, but I lifted a thumb to acknowledge her.

Initially, I visualized the injury being a minor setback. My main concern was, "How hard was the hit?" Once we got settled in the back of the ambulance, I asked one of the paramedics, "Do you think that will be the hit of the week?" He responded, "You really gave it to him. You really rocked him." At that moment, inside the truck, everything felt so right, as if I belonged there. The paramedics were so cautious with me. Everything was so peaceful, and all I could think about was the hit. I laid there with a smile on my face while being transported to the hospital because I knew I was in great hands. I had every intention of playing the next game, finishing the season, leading my team to a state championship, and joining the LSU Tigers in the summer of the following year. Forget the "minor" injury and thumbs up. My mind was still in the game.

The reverberation of that final play is still etched vividly in my mind. On the stretcher ride to the ambulance, I was instructed not to move my neck or my body. Once we made it to the hospital, one of the nurses began cutting my jersey, and that caused pain past describable words. While the nurse cut my jersey, I flashed out and yelled, "What are you doing? I have a game to play next week! Please don't cut my jersey anymore!" She cautiously stared and then proceeded to finish cutting it because they had to do X-rays and an MRI. The entire time my mind was on the field. I wondered who was winning and which plays would make the highlight reel.

Test results put the explosiveness of the play that changed my life forever into perspective. As I laid there in the hospital bed, my parents were standing right next to me, telling me to relax. Then my other guardian angel, Dr. Miguel Melroy, walked in with a shocked look on his face with my test results in his right hand. Before the doctor spoke, he stood there silently examining the X-rays. Then we locked eyes, and he uttered, "How are you alive right now son? You're lucky to be alive!" I still hadn't grasped the magnitude of my injury, so I asked, "What's up doc? What's the diagnosis?" Once again, Dr. Melroy reiterated the fact that I was lucky to be alive, then showed me the X-rays and said, "Your neck is completely broken!" The picture did not resonate with what I always believed, so I questioned the doctor, "If my neck is broken, how am I able to move? How am I able to talk to you doc?" His answer came without hesitation, "You are my miracle child. You were supposed to be dead on that field. God must have been with you."

I instantly knew that the hit was bad from the moment it happened. Hindsight is indeed 2020. Now I can tell you that my neck was broken. At the time, I was figuratively in the dark. In one minuscule second, my dreams and intentions were headed to being unfulfilled. The doctor's words made me feel as though my future placement in the world of football was relegated to fantasy. It was unbeknownst to me when the jersey was cut off of my body that it would be the last time I would ever officially wear a McDonogh 35 football jersey.

The disbelief radiated around the room. My dad is not an emotional person. He passed out his affection sparingly at best or not at all. That night differed. The streaking tears he shed signaled the seriousness of the moment. Even then, my concern was not for my health, but what I left on the field. Call it teenage hubris, but my thought process was simply, how hard did I hit him? I was still in disbelief and not ready to think that my football days were a thing of the past at seventeen-years old.

My injury brought back memories of the story of the actor, Christopher Reeves. Superman broke his neck and was never able to walk again. Would my fate intersect with his? Would I walk again? Run? Play football? The doctor quickly shot down my fear of being confined to a chair. Yes, my injury was like Superman's, but I had no paralysis. I only required surgery to mend the broken neck. In retrospect, I am amazed that the outcome was not worse. Thank God, my fate was not what I feared.

Since the doctor spoke so optimistically about my injury, I assumed the surgery would be uncomplicated, I would be patched up, and then be sent back to my team. We had an opportunity to make the playoffs and possibly win it all. I guess Dr. Melroy did what doctors are trained to do, give hope.

The surgery was scheduled five days after the injury occurred. In the meantime, I was placed in a halo contraption to ensure that my neck and head were stabilized. I will never forget this metal design because I am now branded with two bald spots on both sides of my head that remind me of those days leading up to the surgery. When I saw the halo being brought into my room, I could only imagine the scene from the movie Saw when the character's head was put in the halo, and she had to find a key to get it unlocked. I felt trapped, just like her. As the docs started screwing the metal rods in the sides of my head, all I could do was rattle off curses and screams as my stepmom attempted to calm me down. I wouldn't wish this pain on anybody. I quickly realized it would be a risky procedure. My doctor and surgeons professed that my injury was an anomaly. My medical team had to fuse my C3, C4, C4, C5, C5, and C6 vertebrae's. One wrong move, a centimeter to the left or right, and my story would have taken a different trajectory. I put my faith in God and the team he ordained to see me through the life-threatening situation. Right before surgery, I told the surgeon, "Doc, I'm putting my life in your hands."

Six hours after being wheeled into the operating room, the first part of the procedure was completed. The team went in and fixed my laryngeal prominence, better known as the Adam's apple. I was not out of the woods yet. Four days after a grueling six-hour long operation, I was back under anesthesia in another operating room to move a bone leaning against the internal carotid artery, one of the major vessels that bring blood to the brain. This was another high-risk emergency surgery. If the bone would've punctured the artery at any time between the occurrence of the injury, until the moment it was fixed, my life would have ended instantly. Think of how easily that could have happened with all of those movements. My life would have been a tragic, cautionary tale, but I lived to tell the story.

All of this cutting and mending spoke volumes about the direction my life was heading. Football was not going to be a part of my life in the short-term. I held on to hope and never let it slip too far from my reach. The thoughts of not playing football at the age of seventeen never crossed my mind. Devastation was the best way to sum it up. The moments before surgery and the ones after, it fully dawned on me that football is a game, and my life is more important than any championship, where I would play, or even if I would play next fall.

A month-long hospital stay and the question of whether I would walk again illuminated the reality that I am not invincible. This situation gave me a glimpse of life mostly reserved for those who have lived at least several decades. Still, football was my first love. I loved the game before I even fully understood its rules. It was never far from my heart or mind.

The nurses checked on me 24/7 and made me feel more loved than ever, but my time was still hard in the hospital. Ironically, it felt like I belonged there the entire time. Every time Jasmine visited me, I kept asking about how my team was doing. One Friday night, I got a chance to watch my team blowout a district opponent on the hospital television. All the while I had a catheter inside my penis. It was the worst pain somebody could ever feel.

The confirmation of my love for the game came when I received the all-clear to leave the hospital. Before going home, I had to learn how to walk again. I gave myself five days to learn because it was all mental to me. I couldn't feel sorry for myself because people already showed me sympathy and felt sorry for me. Yes, it may sound like I was harsh on myself, but those were my thoughts.

After three days passed, I was walking again with great energy and high spirits. My nurses couldn't believe it. All I kept saying to myself was, "GOD is real!" I went from potentially being handicapped forever to walking. I was beyond thankful. However, I had another intricate question, so I asked the doctor, "Will I ever play football again doc?" The encouraging response rang loud in my ears and heart. He replied, "Send me Super Bowl tickets when you make it to the Super Bowl!"

Maybe the doctor answered in an affirmative tone to give hope to a kid who dreamed of nothing else but playing football. Regardless, it meant everything. It signified that my dreams would not be deterred and made me hopeful. When someone tells you that you are alive only by the grace of God, the awesomeness of it lingers. It reinforces your convictions and your drive.

The doctor's words reinvigorated my resolve. Whatever came next, I would embrace it with the same determination and zeal I always displayed. I was alive, and the lights momentarily dimmed, but had not gone out.

The broken neck was actually a blessing in disguise. Everything football-related had been going too smoothly. Now I had to fight for everything that I would ever get in this department. I learned how to cherish the failures and celebrate the victories. Every step was a leap of faith, and it had to be done without fear. The broken neck was only a test of my endurance, and I passed.

Chapter 9: Unbroken

My hospital visit lasted for almost one month. I checked in on game day and two days after my birthday, October 27, 2006, and was discharged right before Thanksgiving, on November 24, 2006. My dad did not want me sleeping near anyone else. Therefore, I slept on the couch in the living room where I could be safe from any excess movement. At home, I was going to be treated with kid gloves.

Being relegated to the couch gave me a chance to look retrospectively at what all I had been through. Football gave me my passion. On the field, I had that killer instinct. I was motivated to be positive off the field and did not take my anger issues out on random people on the street. Many people do so, but it was never me. All of my frustration, anger, and bravado was taken out on my opponents. Now here I am, lying on the couch being humbled. I was confident and somewhat big-headed about my abilities, yet I had to live without the beneficial adrenaline rush that playing football gave me. I was not invincible. To no surprise, there was no release of frustration or anger on the couch. I had to rest in the same manner of respectfulness I was taught to give others as I laid on the sofa recovering without projecting any way I felt inside.

I often held on to Dr. Melroy's two positive affirmations during my three week stint on the couch. Being deemed his miracle boy and the opportunity to play football again gave me precisely what I needed to keep fighting. My rehabilitation started with me lifting one-pound dumbbells. Being strong was temporarily part of the past. I watched the movie Rocky and saw myself training like he did to fight. He inspired me, but I didn't go as far as eating raw eggs and so forth. However, I built up slowly and graduated from one pound dumbbells to two pounds and higher. My determination was so strong that I rejoined the school track team three months after being released from the hospital and won a gold medal at the state finals. I knew that I was on my way. I proved my stamina not just to myself but to all of those around me.

I deserved everything I dreamed of and told myself, "It's yours!" after one of my first major athletic milestones post-surgery. I was one of a kind and took the reins of my destiny. The only therapy I had after leaving the hospital was homemade. Grinding was an understatement! My dad was deeply involved in training my brother to prepare him for the upcoming college football season at Ole Miss. I didn't sit out during those workouts because I had all the hopes in the world of being able to play in the upcoming season at LSU.

Around school, I became known as the guy who broke his neck. I do not like pity parties, so of course, I wanted nothing to do with this kind of attention. These trials stopped burdening my mind after I received a phone call I'll never forget.

The Head Coach at LSU, Les Miles called one evening and asked, "How are you doing?" as soon as I answered the phone. I was thrilled to tell him that I was already doing weights and running track. He appeared amazed at my quick recovery process, although he cautioned me about rushing it. Nonetheless, he made my night and changed my life for good when he said, "We still want you at LSU, and we want to offer you a scholarship!" My heart felt as though it took me on a ride through the sky. The fifteen years of blood, sweat, and tears I put in before breaking my neck was strong enough to secure a lifelong dream. Feeling unbroken was an understatement.

Chapter 10: College Is On The Horizon

My journey at LSU started during the spring of 2008. I was set up in a dorm with other athletes. It was an exciting opportunity to get to know my teammates before I began playing with them. I knew I wouldn't get the chance to play the upcoming season because the coach grey-shirted me. That meant I was on the team, but would sit out one year to recover from injuries sustained before arriving. This one year of sitting out would not take away from my four years of eligibility. I was thankful for the opportunity and didn't mind the wait. The next season I would be able to give them 150% of Delvin Breaux and four years of it if needed before turning pro.

Nine months of anxiously waiting for the opportunity to show my teammates what I was made of went by, and it was time for spring training the next year. I was more than ready to play. Because I was grey-shirted, I had to have a medical evaluation and receive clearance from the team doctors before practicing or playing again. I felt fired up and fully healed, but of course, I am not a doctor. This evaluation was their job, and there was no argument about that.

A few days before spring practice I was scheduled to have three individual appointments with the three team doctors. Each doctor would examine me and make their assessment of my preparedness for play.

The first appointment was at 9:00 AM. I walked confidently into the office, feeling no sense of negativity. This first doctor didn't do much talking. He placed a picture of a neck's skeleton in front of me after I sat down. Once he started talking, I saw his mouth moving, but my ears didn't connect with his words. I gained clarity once he said, "You should just take this free education and not worry about football." There was no arguing with his professional opinion. I still had two more doctors to see that afternoon and hoped that it was a game of majority rules.

For the rest of the morning, my thoughts were tied up with what the first doctor said. I knew I did not make it that far to have my dreams curtailed. The first appointment was in and out, and then my next one was at 1:00 PM. I anticipated that the second doctor would say something else, but I was sadly mistaken. It was as if he followed the same script as the first doctor. I was still green to the process and firmly held on to the hope that I'd suit up for the LSU Tigers football team.

My third appointment was at 4:00 PM, and I was cautiously optimistic. This doctor had to tell me what I wanted to hear. This appointment was slightly different. While looking at the picture of the skeleton's neck, he used his index finger to point out the areas of my neck that were injured. The doctor emphasized every word as he reminded me of what a devastating injury I sustained.

What happened to me being the "miracle boy?" I didn't want to hear anything except for, "You are cleared to play!" I zoned out while the third doctor's lips were moving, but I didn't hear a word he was saying, just like the first doctor. The doctor regained my attention when he said, "Son, do you see this picture of the neck up here? It is too dangerous for you to play. You just need to focus on getting an education and put football behind you." The third appointment was far from a charm.

All I kept hearing was, "forget football!" I quietly and rhetorically thought, are they fucking kidding me? That was the final assessment? I grew enraged, and my voice needed to be heard. This is my life and all I ever dreamed of! This is my passion! Someone is going to hear me.

After the doctor voiced the verdict, he did not budge from his stance. He was finished, and I was dismissed. The fighter in me ignited to new heights. Forgetting about football was a life sentence for me that I wasn't going to accept.

I am not proud to say it, but this day sent me on a downward spiral and took me back to the day at nine years old when I picked up the gun in my father's closet. Ironically, these two dates were exactly nine years apart.

No one knew what I did that night. My thoughts differed this time. I planned on taking my life slowly and painfully. My drive and optimistic energy vanished. Not only did I give up, but I wanted to die as well. I had been prescribed Vyvanse for ADHD. After that fateful day, I began mixing my medication with alcohol.

My initial prescription of 60 milligrams was too much and I got it reduced to 30. This showed some glimmer of self-care. My next step with the football program was to begin as a student coach.

I couldn't take more than three days of that role. One of the female athletic trainers took heed to my angst. I didn't say much, but my body language spoke volumes. Once she asked me what was wrong, I broke down and told her that this was not working, and I wanted to play. She heard my pain, but that couldn't alter my heartbreak. Moments after expressing myself, I walked out of the football operations building at LSU and never returned. It was time for my next plan to take effect.

Chapter 11: Downward Spiral

Depressed is too mild of a depiction to express how I felt. Thoughts of ending it all were continuous. I allocated an illogical amount of my scholarship and grant money to self-medicating daily. The pain was nearly unbearable. Six Vyvanse pills and a daily dose of Redberry Cîroc was my prescribed daily fix. I thought I was one of Sean Diddy's son with all of that Cîroc. I could have easily been a brand ambassador for the company. A liquor store close to the campus allowed underage students to buy alcohol and didn't check identification. Drinking was a rite of passage for most college students.

During this timeframe, I was hardly sleeping, and my thoughts were cloudy. Those who saw me when I'd come out of my seven-day stints sequestered in my college apartment commented on my altered appearance. It was evident that I wasn't in football-playing condition anymore. I became frail, and my eyes told the story of what I had been up to. That one day and the words from the mouths of those three doctors got the best of me.

The agony of my childhood trauma, a broken neck, and now being blocked from playing the game that I believed was my future left me little desire to live. I was hoping that this destructive behavior would cause my heart to explode. Although it was obvious that my life took a sharp turn away from what I and others projected, no one cared enough to ask how I was doing while I was at my lowest. The cheering and supportive faces vanished just like my opportunity to play for LSU. There was not one person who was looking out for me at those times.

My only revival came from those frequent talks with my stepmom. She made time to talk to me no matter what time of day I would call. My guardian angel answered the phone every time I called in the wee hours of the morning to vent my depression. I'd ask, "Why me? Why do I have to suffer and endure this pain? What did I do so wrong as a kid?" along with an array of other questions. Only one person could answer most of my questions, but getting him to do that was a pipe dream. I knew God had all the answers for my injury, but my dad felt he raised us the right way, so receiving justification would remain a part of my imagination.

Doing hard time in the prison of my mind caused me to up my dosage of self-medication. Two bottles a day of Redberry Cîroc and those pills could have taken me out at any time. Help was nowhere in sight and no one knew fully about my condition. Not even my stepmom, whom I talked to regularly, nor my dad or my siblings.

What I went through growing up made the thought of going back home outlandish. LSU was supposed to be my next step. College was supposed to prepare me for the NFL draft. How could I return to New Orleans and talk to the one who abused me? What would he do or say to propel me out of this funk? Football was supposed to take me far from that place, but it brought me right back to it.

Chapter 12: Sarah Came To Help Me

I was in dire need of help. Lying in a room alone, drinking and taking pills, would not get me anywhere if I planned to stay alive and healthy. Those were things I didn't care about then. The worst thing about this slow death was constant suffering. I partied here and there, but most of my time was spent in a mentally dark place. An intervention would have been God sent.

During one evening I remember as if it was yesterday, a few college friends invited me out to Hooters. This would be my first time eating there. That alludes to my sheltered upbringing. There were no parties or hanging out until my senior year, and even then, it wasn't anything major or what most high schoolers experienced. I was somewhat reluctant about the Hooters outing, but went anyway.

The host led us to the table where my life would change forever. When the waitress arrived at our table, she locked eyes with me and made it evident that I captured her attention. I planned on ignoring her stares as she took our orders and introduced herself to me as "Sarah." Before she walked past hearing distance, my buddies began encouraging me to take the bait and get her number. I was still uninterested because I was still trying to get myself together. Plus, I wasn't looking for a girlfriend, and never dated outside of my race before. Hanging out for a few and going back to my room was all I planned for that night, and I stuck with it.

During the following week at a party I spotted a familiar face. While maneuvering through the crowd, she caught my attention. Sarah provoked a different reaction outside of her work clothes. While hanging by the keg with my best friend, DJ, I pointed to the girl I told him about that worked at Hooters.

Once she noticed me, I instantly remembered that I didn't leave her a tip. I would have emptied my wallet that night if I had something in it. As soon as she got within arms distance, she reminded me of my uncharacteristic act and said, "Oh, I remember you. You're the guy that didn't leave me a tip!" The anticipated tension turned into instant comfort. Coincidence or not, something un-orchestrated happened, and this was more than just a random occurrence.

I figured friendship would be a great starting place. We exchanged numbers and began a close relationship. This was exactly what I needed at the time. We became quite close, but I knew I did not want to take it too far. However, things started progressing quickly. That small conversation at a party was the seed to a new beginning.

Sarah and I met during the darkest stage of my life when no one else was there. She was enrolled at LSU also and enthusiastically encouraged me not to give up. That was the positive energy I needed to start working out again and regain my mental and physical strength.

Shortly after getting back on the right foot, I received a random call from Dr. Melroy. He called to check in and see why I wasn't playing football. Here I am working on picking up what I left behind, and Dr. Melroy appears out of nowhere to give me an additional shot of much needed adrenalin to continue my momentum. Early into our God-sent conversation he said that he would have been cleared me to play. I'm thinking LSU is not over yet.

With this new burst of encouragement, I went back to the LSU medical facility and into the doctors' offices that would not clear me to play. I figured the doctor's appraisal who performed the surgery would assure the LSU doctors of my ability to play.

I figured wrong. These meetings did not play out the way I would have liked. They only cleared me to work out with weights and run around the track, but nothing involving practicing with the team or anything involving physical contact. The doctors at LSU had no confidence that I could play without sustaining an additional injury to my neck. I was back at square one.

A new thought during April 2010 reinvigorated me. I sought out the coaches at the University of Arkansas Monticello to plead my case for a chance to play on their football team. As soon as I arrived, appointments were made for me with the team's doctors. The LSU doctors wouldn't be able to stop this opportunity.

It worked! All the doctors cleared me to play! Why hadn't I thought of this before? Maybe it was the call from Dr. Melroy or the fact that I was in better shape than a year ago. My hopes were through the roof. This was at the time of the Spring Game which is when college football teams scrimmage in front of their fans. It is here where coaches make depth chart changes. It was perfect timing to interject myself into their minds. So far, it was working. My zeal and optimism had not betrayed me.

Unfortunately, there was a hurdle, and it had nothing to do with a four-year old neck injury. A roadblock existed because of my many dark times at LSU. While I overdid it with prescribed medicine and drank too many pints of Cîroc trying to die, my room became my hidden sanctuary. Going to class or keeping my grades up were last on my list of priorities. I had been dropped from the roll, and my scholarship became non-existent. LSU would not release all of my grades, and some would not transfer over to Monticello. Although my prospective college wanted me to play for them, there was nothing they could do about the grade situation which rendered me ineligible to transfer.

I returned to Baton Rouge with a different mindset. Subconsciously, my attachment to LSU was just as bad as staying home with my dad in New Orleans. It appeared that LSU knew in advance they had no intention of clearing me to play. Each of those doctors' words seemed scripted and identical. It felt like I left New Orleans to walk into the same situation at LSU. I felt rejected and dependent again. The only difference was that I had football to lean on back home, unlike in Baton Rouge.

During this timeframe, my finances were squandered, I got evicted, and Sarah and I became an item. Things with her and I occurred organically. Although she lived with three other people, she still gracefully took me in when I needed a place to stay. With grown man responsibilities on my plate now, I got a job at the Varsity Theater Music Hall as a Bouncer. Sarah was still in school and working part-time at Chimes eatery. It was a pretty nice setup. Chimes subcontracted the clients at the Varsity. When their food orders were taken, they were completed and delivered by Chimes servers. Things were livable and copacetic, but it wasn't what I dreamed of.

Deep inside, I still wanted to play football. I began playing on a flag football team with my friend PJ. He knew about my desire to continue playing ball, and flag football was a way to keep me in shape. I was thrilled to play football even if it was flag. After intercepting four passes in one game, PJ told me that I didn't need to be out there, and he pushed me to play arena football. I responded by telling him, "Give me one year to get in shape, and I promise you I'm going to go give it a try. Until this day, I no longer call him a friend. He's now my brother. PJ put me in the right position to rekindle my dreams and love for the game.

After Sarah graduated from LSU in 2012, she started clinicals at LSUHSC (Health and Science Center), so we moved to New Orleans. I got a job at Subway that lasted all of two weeks.

During training on my first day, I realized it was not for me. I even inquired about dish washing to get away from stacking Subway sandwiches. Have you ever done something contrasting your skill-set or skill-level? Standing up preparing sandwiches on request several hours a day fit the bill for me in that department. Believe it or not, I wasn't fast enough. I was the only man working with an all-woman staff, and they ran circles around my sandwich-making skills. Plus, I kept making mistakes such as too much meat, not enough mayo, or letting the line pile up because I didn't know what I was doing. My tenure came to an end on the fourteenth day when they took my name off the schedule.

We lived on St. Charles Avenue in the Central Business District with our beautiful dog, Diesel, an all-white boxer with a brown patch over his right eye. He reminded people of the dog Pete on Lil Rascals. Our place was right on the Mardi Gras parade route. I landed my second job at Walk-On's sports bar and restaurant as a barback, which was a five-minute walk from the Superdome. Sarah worked with me at Walk-On's as a server. We were now riding the trolley to work, and our LSU days were long behind us.

Being back in my hometown provoked me to visit my high school doctor, Dr. Jagger. Playing football was still at the front of my mind. I wanted to capitalize on the surrounding opportunities. After I expressed my desires to Dr. Jagger, he cleared me to play contact football with the Louisiana Bayou Vipers.

I immediately joined their team, which was a part of the Gridiron Developmental League. My mindset was focused on creating highlight films for the Arena Football League, Canadian Football League, and NFL scouts. It was a road less traveled, but not impossible for those who can imagine a greater future. There are some comical takeaways from the smorgasbord of players. The players on the sideline consisted of characters drinking beers and smoking cigarettes while waiting for their opportunity to get in the game and others who didn't take the game seriously. However, that didn't alter my focus, energy, and effort. If anything, it gave me fuel to stay on course. These sideline sceneries may not have been serious, but I was.

By now, several years went by since I played one down of tackle football. It was almost time to break that drought. It was like riding a bike, and I was ready to strap on the pads under the bright lights again. Dr. Jagger became held in my highest regard, just as Dr.

Melroy. I am forever thankful for them speaking life into my career and never doubting my comeback.

Chapter 13: Daylight

My first game with the Bayou Vipers was an away game in Florida. Nervous was an understatement. Flag football is a different beast from contact football. The Gridiron League was semi-pro. Some of these guys had something to prove and I did also. The Vipers and the opposing team were going to see the Breaux Show in full effect on this beautiful day in Florida.

My first action occurred on the second play of the game when the running back came rumbling in my direction. I met him full force when I turned my head to the side and made the tackle. I emptied my lungs in excitement after delivering my first hit in four years. It felt like I made the game-winning tackle in the Super Bowl. My mind mustered the thoughts, "They done messed up and let me play! The Breaux Show is back baby!!!"

At the conclusion of my first season, I was voted an All-Star. It was ironic, but staying in shape with flag football, playing semi-pro, and training at Velocity with dedicated trainers and former NFL players, put me back in the game and formed me into an All-Star.

My football life was anything but easy since I broke my neck in October of 2006. God always knew my strength, heart, and character, and gave one of the hardest battles to one of his toughest soldiers. My dark times did not permanently take away my passion for living life to the fullest. The low times made me even more grateful. Unexpected occurrences and unpredictable manifestations gave me reassurance when I felt things were spiraling out of control.

Protecting others came naturally, so my job as a bouncer aligned more with my natural skill-set than making six-inch or foot-long cold cut sandwiches. I viewed it as overseeing everything to ensure everyone was safe, and I spent an entire year doing something desirable outside of football. For the rest of my life, I will continue being a protector.

I have been fortunate enough to run into the right people who were at the right place at the right time. When Sarah and I moved to New Orleans, we were obviously not rolling in dough. Our house had issues that many older homes do, including a roach problem and other undesirable living conditions. The washing and dryer machine's payment slots were broken in the shed of the housing apartment, so we had free laundry.

The drawback of that perk was the tribe of flying cockroaches by the entrance. Nonetheless, it was home, and our landlord was God sent. When money came in, we'd pay three to four months of rent in advance. Occasionally, we fell behind with the rent, but our landlord didn't keep a tight track of our records. We had to leverage that to get by some months when our money ran low.

My paychecks didn't equate to the hard work I put in at Walk On's. That job proved my dependability because I busted my ass all week for a $60 check. While working at Walk-On's, I would see football games on television and tell the staff, "I'm going to be on television playing football one day!"

Maybe because I gave the job all I had, my co-workers believed in me. They'd tell me things like, "You can do it!" and "Go for it!" I pushed myself past exhaustion while striving for my goals and vowed to keep going. There was no stopping me. Sarah pushed me, my co-workers pushed me, and my boss believed in me. I vowed to never take my Subway and Walk-On's days for granted and developed the highest level of respect for employees in those industries. These people are real heroes and those jobs taught me valuable lessons that will stick with me forever.

What I visualized for myself functioned as a vision board sitting at the front of my mind. The vision of the future is what kept me alive. I knew I had to leverage more than my athletic skills to make it to the league. After hard days of work and training, I began relentlessly searching for an agent. Most nights, I searched until my eyes and body gave out, or 4:00 AM. I wrote hundreds of unread emails. The abundance of no's and no responses left me unbothered. Getting tired reassured me that I was on the correct path and almost there.

The emails I wrote spilling my heart out finally caught someone's attention. AG, an agent adviser whose job at the time was to match athletes with agents, began working immediately on my behalf. Although he wasn't a legal agent yet, his engrossment and energy made me want him as my agent. I didn't have money at the time, but AG plugged me in with Velocity Sports in Mid-City, New Orleans to intensify my training. The camaraderie was something I missed about the game. I had many sources of inspiration around me. Numerous other athletes were striving for the next level. My trainer Isaac, Nikky, a former bodybuilder, and friend Big Chief, helped me get acclimated to the new facility and gave me special encouragement. Things felt like destiny when Big Chief introduced me to Ray, a former DB for the Buffalo Bills. Receiving training from someone who played my position in the league was the icing on the cake.

It was great playing flag football and semi-pro, but I refused to stop there. The next step to more was the opportunity to perform at the NFL combine that year. AG and Paramount Associations made it happen. I trained as if I was preparing for the Super Bowl. I jumped a 37" inch vertical and ran a 4.38 in the 40 yard dash. Coaches from the Cincinnati Bengals, Oakland Raiders, and Cleveland Browns plus Arena Football League (AFL) scouts wondered who I was. They all approached me with questions such as, "Who are you?"

and "Where did you come from?" When I said my name and mentioned McDonogh 35, they recognized me as the player who broke his neck as a senior and former LSU prospect. They all thought I quit football after my devastating injury.

The professionals' consensus at the combine recommended that the AFL would be best for me at the time. This was a more traveled route to the NFL than the Gridiron League. Making another step closer to my ultimate goal assured me that the AFL was the right move. These scouts and coaches knew talent when they saw it. I left the combine with high hopes. My progressive actions rubbed off on AG and inspired him to obtain his requirements to become an agent. My first scheduled workout was with the Utah Blaze of the AFL, but I did not sign with them because I wanted to keep my options open. Before I could open my suitcase when I returned home, I received a call from the AFL team, the New Orleans Voodoo.

Chapter 14: Canada

After one year with the Vipers, I signed with the New Orleans Voodoo. Three games into the season, a labrum tear in my right shoulder landed me on injured reserve. When my shoulder was fully rehabilitated, it created an opportunity for other teams to sign me.

The Hamilton Tiger-Cats of the Canadian Football League (CFL) called me in for a workout and the opportunity to play at a higher level. Voodoo Head Coach O'Hara and Defensive Back Coach Ward congratulated me and told me to go for it.

Before I knew it, I chartered a first-class plane ride to San Mateo, California. I dominated the workout, which consisted of 200+ players. After the auditions were over, the coaches declared that I was not leaving without signing. Other CFL teams, including the Edmonton Eskimos and Winnipeg Bluebombers, were interested, but the Tiger-Cats seemed to be the best fit. I was the only person at the California camp who signed a deal with the team. My steps felt ordered by the highest power, and I was finally a professional athlete.

My flight to Canada three months after my workout gave me a different set of butterflies than the California trip. The excitement was beyond words while I clutched my passport and chewing gum at the New Orleans Airport before takeoff. It was as if the plane departing from Louis Armstrong Airport took me to heaven. The people in Canada impressed me immediately. The city that I never imagined stepping foot in was a different world. While leaving the airport, I accidentally bumped into a man, and he issued a mutual apology. I was prepared for a negative interaction or a scrunched face, but he offered neither and helped welcome me to my new home.

My social skills paid off, and I instantly made two friends, and we instantly became jointed at the hip. If you saw one, you saw the other two. This sealed my comfortability and eased the transition to a new country and a new team.

In 2013, I had a "welcome to the league" moment when I got scored on in a tight game against our heated rivals, the Toronto Argonauts, during the final seconds of a game we lost. We had another opportunity to score, but we didn't seal the deal. I took responsibility and shouldered the reason for our loss. The embarrassment ate me alive the whole bus ride home, but I had to brush it off and get ready for next week.

Even though I was finally playing professional football, the ambiance wasn't what I imagined. It felt like I was living in solitary confinement between practices and games. Staying in a hotel past one week is a different experience than a place to lay your head on vacation. Those four white walls of my room in the Crowne Plaza where I lived for six months began caving in on me. Being 1100 miles away only made the velocity of the caving in walls increase. Hess Street, which consisted of bars and restaurants where college students went, was the only thing to do in Hamilton. My circumstances forced me to grow up quickly. The coaches and staff didn't provide much help to the players on the 46-man roster. Therefore, we were propelled into the real world and forced to figure things out on the fly.

An intricate part of being a professional is maintaining your confidence while learning from your mistakes.

Things trended upward after my first game. I contributed to my team making the Grey Cup (CFL Super Bowl/Championship) while battling a torn labrum in my left shoulder. We lost badly, but making it there was quite an accomplishment. I racked up 27 tackles and one sack in nine games. I was scheduled for another hospital visit at the end of the season to repair my left shoulder injury I suffered with the New Orleans Voodoo. It sucked because I had to be in a sling for a couple of weeks with a nerve ball attached to me, but I'm glad I got it repaired because I needed my all for the mission at hand.

During my second year, I was voted a CFL All-Star and East Division All-Star. The second stint in Canada was much better because Sarah and our dog Diesel joined me. I told Sarah I couldn't do it by myself again. Also, I couldn't do living in a hotel again neither.

We moved to the mountains in a stranger's basement. Sarah made a smooth transition and enhanced my Canadian experience. She quickly established friendships, plus joined a flag football and frisbee league, which gave me something to do after practice. I loved seeing her play and enjoy herself.

Having a partner by my side awarded me the opportunity to enjoy the nuances of Canada aside from football. Breathtaking sights of Niagara Falls somewhat compensated for the childhood vacations I never experienced. That exposure opened my eyes to the importance of traveling and seeing the world. Canada is a place I highly recommend visiting. Toronto, which is only thirty minutes away from where I resided, consists of some of the most beautiful people and scenery this earth has to offer. Seeing the high level of diversity in Toronto was something that warmed my heart because we are all one, and love provokes life's best features.

No matter where a New Orleanian steps foot on earth, their accent always stands out. I must have received a million requests to say the word baby, and I happily obliged to each one with a warm smile. It was an honor to consistently be a reflection of my beloved city and contribute to another person's smile.

My arena league experience helped me adjust to the CFL and provide valuable training for my teammates that hadn't experienced such rules.

The rules and field in the CFL are different from the NFL, but closely resemble arena football. The CFL's field is 150 yards long and 65 yards wide, and the NFL's field is 100 yards long by 53 ½ yards wide. Instead of 11 players on the field during an NFL game, the CFL allows 12. Three receivers in the CFL were allowed to get a running start behind the line of scrimmage before the snap. The NFL doesn't permit such movement and holds a shorter season, versus the CFL who's season persists of an 18 game season on a 21-week regular season. Also, there are three downs instead of four like in the NFL.

As a defensive player, I got all my bad repetitions out of the way while playing in the AFL. Mirroring the foot-speed of wide receivers is no easy task, but I rose to the occasion on every snap. Facing them with a running start didn't intimidate me. Helping my teammates get adjusted helped me build everlasting bonds and friendships. Those type of connections are one of the most gratifying elements of sports.

We made the Grey Cup again during my second season and lost in a better fashion. The game dramatically slipped out of our hands in the final moments when a last-minute penalty negated a touchdown ran back by one of the fastest players in the league. Before that play, I made an acrobatic interception that swung the momentum in our favor. The loss hurt, but it left me hungry for more. At the end of the season, I made the all-star team and garnered the interest of 28 NFL teams.

Chapter 15: It's Breaux Show Time

Before I got settled back in Baton Rouge, Louisiana, after my second CFL season, my agent, Gary Stevens, called to give me the breakdown of the next steps. Auditioning for NFL teams began immediately. There was no time for a restful winter break and recovering from an 18-game season of professional football. It was time to get busy! I shoved the pain and fatigue to the side and was fired up to show the NFL what I was working with.

I tried out for the Houston Texans, New England Patriots, Arizona Cardinals, Minnesota Vikings, Jacksonville Jaguars, Tampa Bay Buccaneers, Denver Broncos, San Francisco 49ers, San Diego Chargers, Seattle Seahawks, Pittsburgh Steelers, Miami Dolphins, Indianapolis Colts, and Detroit Lions.

These workouts took place in rapid succession with no room to breathe before Christmas. I zigzagged across the country from one workout to the next. After killing each and every workout, no team cleared me for play. I could not believe this shit and my time felt wasted. Why was I working out? Each team was familiar with my history, so I assumed getting cleared wouldn't be an issue. Christmas arrived, but my NFL contract didn't.

Thankfully, there were still fifteen more teams who wanted to see me. Next up was the Atlanta Falcons, my hometown team's arch-rival. The competitive nature of their rivalry crept off the field and into the front office. Once the Saints got wind of my workout with the Falcons, they intercepted my workout plans and called me in to tryout. My hometown team requested a switch that was readily granted. After all those shut-downs, I felt confident about the New Orleans Saints. The other teams drawing the same excitement I bestowed for the Saints was impossible.

I was ready to work out the moment I heard that my hometown team wanted to see me! I repeatedly thanked God and couldn't get my feet in a pair of cleats fast enough. Out of the millions of workouts I did throughout my entire career, I was most prepared for the one with the Saints and felt a special surge of energy.

The day of the workout was as beautiful as the opportunity ahead of me. I killed the first part of the workout by catching everything thrown my way and running a 4.48 in the 40-yard dash. The Head Coach of the Saints was the main person I intended to impress, but he wasn't on the field to watch me and the other two players workout.

When he did join us on the field, he requested to see something else from me. He watched all three of us workout, but I felt he paid special attention to me. Once I completed the drills, I went in alone to shower and get dressed.

While in the facility waiting to hear if I made it or not, a player on the team came in and said, "You're legit!" My poise remained militant until I grew starstruck when the Head Coach approached and welcomed me to the team.

He and other coaches enthusiastically affirmed my skills, stature, and how I was suited to become an NFL cornerback. This caused me to hold my head high with a strong sense of self-assuredness and gratefulness for everything I experienced en-route to achieving my life-long goal of making it to the NFL.

Sarah's hands were clenched on the gate when I emerged from the facility. I ran to where she stood and wrapped my arms around her, then happily yelled, "I told you I was going to do it!" The fourteen no's I received was worth the one yes. No other team could have offered me a more gratifying opportunity than the Saints. Only a few years prior, my job was to clean up behind bartenders a few blocks away from where I would be paid to play the game I love at the highest level. The manner in which the Saints reeled me in with the organization served as the icing on the cake. They got in the way of a division rival for my services and made me feel wanted.

The contract was prepared for my signature in January. The rookie training camp started several months later on April 18, 2015. My emotions were in full force due to successfully signing with my hometown NFL team. I got married and purchased a house during this timeframe and did not conceptualize the magnitude of the decisions. Things happen in the blink of an eye when you are caught up in the moment.

Sarah envisioned being married by 26 and pregnant at 27. The moment felt right, and I wasn't prideful about putting her needs first because she pulled me from my darkest moments when barely anyone else extended a hand. Our bond propelled me to the highest level, and I would never regret it. Taking our time may have been more beneficial, but new beginnings represented the element and theme of the environment in 2015.

Chapter 16: The League

My rookie moment in the CFL primed me to avoid rookie moments during my first year in the NFL. A potential one presented itself when I lined up against the legendary wide receiver, Steve Smith, during our first game of the season against the Baltimore Ravens.

As soon as I lined up against him, he yelled to his quarterback, "I got a rookie over here!" It was an awkward feeling being disrespected by a person I had the utmost respect for. However, my feelings fade for good once I put a helmet on. I figured he could get it just like anyone else who lines up against me.

Thankfully, I avoided making rookie mistakes, and he didn't get the best of me as he did most cornerbacks he lined up against throughout his highly successful NFL career. Facing an elite team and guarding a household name gave me quite the introduction to the league and intensified my plans to do big things.

I wasted no time emerging myself as a top-ranked corner in the NFL. My success may have caught some people by surprise, but my ability to adapt and perform was what I expected plus I identified more opportunities to improve.

I started every game, snatched three interceptions, recorded 45 tackles, and was rated as a top corner in the league. However, I didn't make the Pro Bowl. Personally, I felt snubbed and was confident in my belief that I was the best cornerback in the league. If a top performer doesn't feel that they are the best at what they do, they are susceptible to getting surpassed by a hungrier person intentionally striving to be the best.

It was said that the number of touchdowns I allowed may have been the reason for being overlooked. I didn't buy it because I checked more boxes off in other areas than some talented ballers with household names who made it. Albeit it being my first year, I knew my lack of popularity might have been my indictment on not making the Pro Bowl, but that knock wasn't strong enough to stop my drive. I had it in my heart to turn the Breaux Show up to new heights the upcoming season.

Although I didn't get the accolade I initially hoped for, I received a piece of hardware that touched the deepest places of my heart. My peers and the Saints staff members selected me as the Ed Block Courage Award winner, which is awarded to one person on each NFL team that displayed the highest level of inspiration, sportsmanship, and courage and carried themselves as a role model. Receiving the award in Baltimore, Maryland, topped off the storybook year.

My entire offseason was dedicated to returning at a higher level the next year. Everything was raised a few levels, including my training, confidence, and even my diet. I walked into the season in top condition, ranked as one of the top cornerbacks in the league, and ready for what was in front of me.

Our first game was against the Oakland Raiders. I couldn't wait for the game to start and wanted to make a statement as early as possible. On a routine punt return a running back's knee caught my fibula and caused me to limp off the field after the play. The pain didn't feel like one I could just shake off.

I took two Toradols, which are powerful non-steroidal anti-inflammatory pills, before the game, as many players do to play through injuries. The pills numbed my pre-existing aches and ailments until the collision. Something didn't feel right, but my mind was locked in on the current mission, the Oakland Raiders.

At half-time, I took two more Toradols. My body reacted like I only ingested two placebo pills. While attempting to get myself together on the sideline, the Head Coach kept asking, "You're not going to quit on your team, are you?" I replied, "I am trying my best to keep going." He responded, "I need my best defensive back."

My injury didn't respond while replying to coach, but I still trotted out there once he yelled, "Come on Breaux!" My body disagreed with the coach's order. I wondered, "What did I have to do to prove that I was really hurt?" Before I knew it, the ball was headed my way. What would have normally been an interception hit my hands then popped out.

I knew I was done, but my heart was stronger than my aching fibula. The applied pressure caused me to play through three more downs on my injury. My game ended once I made a tackle, and the excruciating pain went to new heights once I hit the ground.

The magnitude of my injury caused Derek Carr, the opposing team's starting quarterback, to check on me while I laid in dismay. That meant everything to me because the people who were supposed to care the most were neglectful of my well-being to benefit their own. Winning means the world to me also, but the line must be drawn at some point. I will always have a special place in my heart for coaches, fans, and others who understand that athletes are humans and not machines.

Shortly after being carted off the field, my x-ray revealed a broken left fibula. Once I got the news of how many games I would miss, I couldn't help but think about how the outcome would have been if I didn't go against my will and follow the coach's orders to keep playing on the injury.

During the seven weeks I missed, I understood why patience is a virtue. The team placed me on injured reserve (IR) and scheduled me to return during the eighth week of the season. An overlooked aspect of scheduled return dates from injuries is the lack of available time to regain conditioning. Those return dates are typically set when players can bear enough pain to perform and aren't assigned because they are fully healed. Simultaneously balancing resting my injury and training to hit the field again presented itself as a challenge in such a short timeframe. The staff took heed to that notion and assured me that I would only play twenty-two snaps during my first game back.

While feeling 50% recovered from my broken fibula and on a twenty-two snap count during my first game back, the coaches kept me on the field for 45+ snaps. Week 1 of the season taught me a lesson about being vocal about my condition. Therefore, I told the Head Coach and Defensive Coordinator that I felt 50% recovered. Both verbally agreed in my presence that my 50% is better than most other player's 100%. I am not sure if they said that to affirm my skills, but that sentiment put into perspective their respect for my well-being.

Regardless of my feelings inside, it was drilled into me with a belt to respect authority, and I always did whatever my coaches asked. The coaches painted the picture that they'd slowly work me back into things to get adjusted. The only adjustment I got during my first game back was the readjustment to the pain I felt during week one.

By the third quarter, my leg felt as if it was about to fall off, so I took myself out of the game. My projected snap count was exceeded before halftime, and they showed no signs of pulling me out anytime soon. Once I returned to the sidelines, the Head Trainer began applying heat treatments to my injury. While I grimaced in pain, the Head Coach yelled to the trainer at the top of his lungs, "Get the fuck away from him! He's ok!"

That statement and energy set the tone for my recovery process. I felt like a powerful luxury vehicle that had been in a wreck, needed an oil change, a new bumper, on two donuts being driven in the left lane. After my fourth game back and fourteenth game of the season, I shut down. An AC (acromion) shoulder sprain concluded my 2016 - 2017 season.

God always found a way to incorporate some brightness in the darkness during low points in my life. The brightest light of them all shined and entered the earth on April 10, 2017, when Sarah gave birth to Delvin Breaux, Jr.

Chapter 17: Are You Serious?

Fatherhood made some real things come full circle. Stones felt unturned with my father. All of my off-season preparations consisted of working out with my father leading up to high school. However, he was absent for all the off season workouts post-high school. Consequently, the main thing we bonded over was no longer a mutual activity. While our interactions drifted, the thoughts in my head about my childhood remained. My questions needed answers, and he was the only person who could answer them.

Momentarily, I was unsure about my father's potential response if I reached out. It was season three for me in the NFL, and I just became a father to my namesake, so I was open-minded to new areas of growth. Training with my father presented an opportunity to potentially kill two birds with one stone.

I pushed my pride aside and reached out to my dad for help with my workouts. While dialing his number, I was hornswoggled that I built up enough strength to call him. Once I heard his voice, I knew he could help improve my game and answer much-needed questions to give me some closure about my childhood. Some comforting words from him may have eased those wounds.

I spent three workouts disguising my ulterior motives. During those sessions, I received the basics of my dad's methods, but I didn't accomplish my main objectives. I asked open-ended questions and initiated open conversations with him, but he shut down everything non-football related. Besides breaking down the training moves, he had nothing to say. Meeting up somewhere after training was also a no go. He always had an excuse for not meeting with me other than for workouts. I even invited him to sit with me at Starbucks, but he redirected the conversation to a busted AC in his house.

It was time to cut the training off with him when my other efforts were ignored, and it was evident I would only receive half of what I came for. I didn't regret reaching back out to my dad to work through our issues. Sometimes the only person who can give us closure is ourselves.

The injury I experienced during the first game of the previous season lingered throughout the offseason and preparation efforts for the 2017-2018 season. I knew that wasn't something the coaches wanted to hear at the start of training camp, so I made plans to fight through it.

During practice on the third day of training camp, a player cut back on a play, and his knee banged my fibula that was broken the previous year. At this point, my body felt like it was New Orleans Saints' property. While experiencing this suppression, I was at the mercy of the training and coaching staff.

I don't have an injury barometer in my head, but I knew this one ranked at the top of the severity scale. To my surprise, the team doctors diagnosed my injury as a bone contusion, which in lament terms, means a simple bruise. It was as if a math teacher attempted to tell me $2 + 2 = 22$. Although it was my body, what weight would my word hold against theirs?

It's imperative to pay more attention to patterns than apologies. Not that I ever received an apology for how

I was negligently handled, I knew what to expect next. It wasn't long into my rehabilitation process that the coaches pressured me to return to the field. The Head Coach regularly consulted with the training staff about my injury, but never engaged in dialogue with me about it. This confirmed that my body was New Orleans Saints' property, even though they expressed that sentiment several times before.

It was a hollowing feeling to conceptualize that you are only an object to a person and company. I rehabbed with the training staff as hard as humanly possible. Although nothing seemed to work, it was time to go back to work.

Mental manipulation became a part of the game when the Head Coach told me that my teammates agreed with him that I was playing up my injury. At the time, I was so caught up in the shuffle that I took the bait. I respectfully approached several of my teammates about it. However, they denied it. The Head Coach's demeanor shifted almost every time we crossed paths. It was unfortunate because my injuries caused our relationship to sour. His energy toward me spread to others and some people passed me funny looks as well, but no one spoke on it except for him. The Head Coach's favorite time to talk down on me was in front of my teammates. His lashings out at me reminded me of my father's treatment during my childhood. My brothers checked on me when my dad whipped me harder than them. My teammates did the same after the Head Coach would embarrass me in front of them.

I pretended like everything was fine, but what grown man would or better yet, what human would be ok with what was going on? Hate is a word I intentionally avoid using, but that's the only word to describe how I felt going to work every day enduring the blatant disrespect I received.

"Breaux, you just don't want to practice?" became one of the Head Coach's main punch lines. His favorite place to throw that jab was in the training room while having my leg worked on. At one point, even the starting quarterback and another DB asked about my status, and I echoed the same rebuttal I kept telling the Head Coach. I looked at the quarterback deeply in the eyes and said, "I'm hurting." The notion of me not wanting to practice goes against everything I ever stood for.

Shit hit the fan at full force once the Head Coach and I met at the Hilton Hotel off Airline Highway in Kenner. He dismissively threatened to trade me to Dallas. At this point, I had already been dragged to levels I vowed to never stoop to. I barked back, "Trade me then. Dallas is a beautiful place! I'll help them win a Super Bowl and make the Pro Bowl there!" Sometimes we are antagonized to provoke a specific reaction. He didn't get the one he intended to get out of me, and that changed his tone. I vehemently said, "What do you want me to do? I am really hurt man!" and continued venting. After I called him man several times, he pounded his fist on the desk in front of him and hollered, "If you call me man one more time!" "Then, what are you going to do?" I responded. We restrained ourselves from escalating this altercation. As soon as I got the opportunity and tempers cooled, I told him I wanted a second opinion about my injury. He complied because he believed that outside doctors would confirm the in-house Doctors' diagnosis.

The Saints made an appointment with my trusted doctor, Dr. Shelling, Jr. He was a doctor at Tulane Hospital in Downtown, New Orleans. Our relationship dated back to high school when he stood on the sidelines for some of my games. I knew this second opinion was going to vindicate me.

Once Dr. Shelling, Jr. x-rayed my leg, he returned with a smile. Then he pointed to the x-ray screen and said, "Your leg is broken!" What the team doctors claimed they didn't see was in plain sight. I didn't understand how someone could know my track record and question my toughness. Plus, my public track record isn't even half of the adversity I overcame. My will to fight back from a broken neck should speak volumes about my desire and love for playing the game. I was still willing to run through a brick wall for the game and my team, but I couldn't do that on a broken leg or fibula. With all the years I spent shedding blood, sweat, tears, surgeries, and hustling to make it this far, faking isn't sensible, and quitting is not in me.

I played on a broken leg, but no one cared. The break could have easily turned into a compound fracture bearing my body's weight while I continued playing. The Head Coach never asked another question again after Dr. Shelling, Jr. officially revealed that it was more than just a simple contusion.

One day during a team meeting after my actual injury was revealed, the Head Coach had a few things to get off his chest and an announcement to make. He gave a general account of his errors during the 2009 Super Bowl season and announced that two team doctors were fired. He privately and vaguely spoke to me later, but concluded the meeting without offering a sincere apology in front of the team. When he assumed I was faking, he was boisterous about promoting his campaign that I was milking and exaggerating my injuries.

After the truth was revealed, the apology wasn't as loud as the disrespect. The firing of the team doctors did nothing to float my boat. He continued talking about their mistakes, rolled them under the bus, made them the fall guys, and never took accountability for his actions as I assumed he would.

My teammates called a players' only meeting after the Head Coach wrapped up. Once we finished the meeting, many of my teammates turned to me and said, "don't accept that," as they gave me hugs and daps on the way out. On media day, when sports reporters inquired about my status, players spoke up on my behalf. While I was on the sidelines, the coach began browbeating me. One time after arriving for practice, he told me, "Your teammates are losing faith in you."

Dr. Shelling said that my fibula broke at least a week and a half before it was x-rayed a second time. The pressure forced me to succumb, and I practiced just to prove I was hurt. The psychological trauma that I grew up with was in full effect. I walked, practiced, and withstood the pain of rehab on a broken fibula.

Being quiet was the way mostly all players made it even when they were hurt. If you went against the grain, you could lose pay or lose it all. In result, the culture socially engineers players to suck it up and keep quiet. I tried that for as long as I could. The closed mouth and playing on a broken leg could only be stopped with my demand for a second opinion. This forced me to wonder how many other ballers experienced the same thing and didn't get a chance to articulate their side of the story.

Chapter 18: Went Back to Finish

Breaking a generational curse fixed the anguish of beginning two consecutive seasons on IR with a broken fibula. That speaks volumes about how much I love my son and think the world of him. The dynamics of my injury situation wouldn't have been the same if my injuries weren't avoidable.

I felt two different pain levels when I first got hurt versus when I re-injured myself both times. I tried to take myself out of both games when the initial injuries occurred and re-injured myself even worse after being forced to go back out. I can't help but wonder what could have been if I was handled with respect. The same thought also prepared me for the light that would help me see the world differently.

Many days while under the wing of my father, I dreamed about being able to love a child how I wanted to be loved. As I grew older, I developed more of an understanding of my father's plight, although it did not alleviate me from holding him accountable for how he treated me. Once I began learning what I did not want to do as a father, I realized no one was there to teach him how to be a dad. I can't imagine what he felt like when he was ignored by his father for Soul Train during their first opportunity to meet. Some scars leave an unspoken lifetime mark on us. My dad was an active parent and laid a foundation for us to succeed in life. I took heed to what I liked and disliked because I wanted to be an even better parent than a football player, although I am passionately determined at being the best at both.

While going through surgery after surgery, I wasn't sure about my ability to reproduce, but Delvin Jr. proved that wrong. While I watched him develop in Sarah's stomach and transition from crawling to walking, he inspired me to grow simultaneously. Everything in my heart and soul will ensure that my son experiences a different set of circumstances than I did. I see him as a mini-me. He is beautiful, smart, a reflection of me, and I could not be more pleased that he is my son. I will never resort to physical abuse or intimidation while raising the biggest piece of my heart.

Sometimes we must take one step back to take two steps forward. Well, in my case, two steps back to take three steps forward. Both of my big dreams dissolved at the same time. However, both avenues bridged a way to a better life and added to my legacy. I was bound to lose a body part at the rate I was going with the Saints, and they gave up believing in me for misperceived assumptions while I existed under their reign.

By the end of the season, my leg recovered. However, I was far from healed as a man. I knew that when I agreed to get married. A person isn't adequately prepared for love if they are in the stages of relearning how to love themselves. That was the season I was in when Sarah entered my life. The amount of genuine love, value, and effort she poured into me made me give her my undivided attention for nearly a decade. Her being there for me while I was struggling to find my way and finally making it with her by my side made marriage seem like the prescribed route. Although our bond developed over time, some of our roadblocks were inevitable. Our cultural differences provided a disconnect, and I couldn't fully open up or feel comfortable no matter how hard I tried. It still felt as though it was her and I against the world while we were together. Sarah knew my situation was not ideal, but she bridged the gap from my life's downward trajectory to my destiny. The marriage ended, but I will always be grateful for what Sarah and I accomplished together.

Way before the divorce, I had a moment of clarity and decided to be painfully honest with Sarah. One day I wrote her a letter spilling my heart about where I stood. I still could not help but think of how she came into my life at the right time. She was there to pull me through. There were certain moments when we were all good. Everything was right in the world. She motivated me to go after and capture my dreams. I couldn't imagine another person knowing what I went through but still expecting me to rise above the circumstances. She comforted me when I was in dark spaces. We never had any physical altercations. We were in each other's lives for powerful reasons. My letter to Sarah elaborated on how I felt, but it did not change how I would treat her going forward. The divorce was inevitable, but I am eternally grateful for her being there.

We remained together for nine years. During that time, Sarah tolerated my dark moods, drinking, memory loss, and surrounding chaos in my life. She handled it like a champ and deserves an applause. I was loyal and grateful to be with her. Not only did she help redeem the time I lost, but she also gave me my greatest gift, Delvin Breaux, Jr.

By December 2017, we called it quits, and shortly after, the Saints released me. The marriage ended amicably. Sarah knows I will do all of what I promised. I want my son to have all of his needs and the love I never had. In May 2018, the Hamilton Tiger Cats of the CFL called for me once again.

I made the Eastern and Canadian Football League All-Star team my first year back, then signed a three-year deal and became the highest-paid cornerback in the league. I lived up to the contract. The Breaux Show was in full effect for the 2019 - 2020 season and I made the All-Star team again. The CFL has been good to me, and I am greatly appreciative for it.

My life experiences have truly humbled me. I made it through all of this, and I'm still here stronger, sharper, wiser, and more prepared for life's journey. Most are clueless about what goes on behind the scenes of professional football unless they've been told first-hand. Even then, there are still more unspoken nuances to experience. Thankfully, not many ballers can say they have endured my level and volume of trials and tribulations. However, many players still haven't recovered from their respective pain due to the game's mental and physical rigors.

Unanimously, research shows that NFL players are more prone to health issues after their playing days are over. I chose this sport and knew in advance the abuse my body would endure. However, I didn't forecast the neglect and disrespect I endured. If players experience health issues, especially cognitive, they should at least be given every benefit of the doubt. The NFL is finally taking note of the results from multiple concussions. I aim to shed light on emotional trauma that's swept under the rug. It is all a major blow to overall health.

Making peace with my experiences has always been my goal. I'm still on the journey to complete that mission, but I want to bring awareness so that it does not happen to others. If one coach changes from reading this, I have made some impact. Being a professional athlete is a gift and an anomaly. Many players who came up short have left the league with a broken spirit and disappeared into the past, never to be spoken about again.

God doesn't close one door without opening up another. The CFL offered me an opportunity to continue playing. Although I'd be heading back to Canada, I was still mindful of what happened while in the NFL. Yes, doctors were fired, but my reputation was altered to other players, fans, and organizations. How else could a player go from being a top ranked cornerback in the league to not being signed by another team when made available? If other teams would have known the truth then, I know in my heart that I wouldn't have been headed back to Canada again. Regardless of what could have been said then, there wasn't a way to voice the truth without consequences.

Was there a character flaw with one coach, or was the issue something that happens regularly? I'm grateful for professional football, but wish to spark a change regarding relationships between coaches and players. I am hopeful that someone in authority hears my heart and understands the message I am conveying. Players are human beings, and coaches should be reminded of this. Winning is everything to some coaches, and I understand that, but they should not win at the expense of some players leaving the game permanently wounded.

Sometimes we must be thankful for our own problems. I know I experienced the dream of many others by playing in the NFL, along with other perks of being a football standout. However, look at what all I encountered along the way. A broken neck in twelfth grade, a left fibular that was broken two years in a row, and a childhood living in survival mode is only a gist of my story. I was built for the low points and made it out. My life has not been a cautionary tale. This is my story and what I have been through makes me unique. I am beyond appreciative for that.

Chapter 19: A Promising Start

Our family's trauma has rendered us as a family nearly irreparable. I can only hope for better in the future and remain optimistic. My stepmom and I still have a relationship and keep in touch. The pain still burns deeply. I know how much I have been hurting, but I know that the New Orleans East cannot hold many fond memories for any of us, including my stepmom.

Henry and I have gained enough strength to finally talk about those days when our dad abused us. While it was happening, there was nothing funny about it because we had no clue if or when it would ever stop. Now we let our imaginations run wild with thoughts of what we could have done back then. My brothers and I were physically imposing enough to put a halt to his terror, but mentally we were still subjected children. Henry, Brandon, and I jokingly beat ourselves up for not thinking about how we could have defended ourselves against the onslaught of a man who had never been taught how to love.

My dad inflicted and recycled what my grandmother projected on him. He was abused, and in turn, he abused us. He did not seek other ways to discipline his children, although he had to be tormented about his own treatment by his mother and neglect of his father. I successfully ended two generational curses. At least "nearly irreparable" means there is still a chance for some degree of healing.

Strange as it is, joking about painful memories made my brothers and I bond deeper. This is how I know sharing is therapeutic. Venting with my loved ones encouraged me to open up about my story and contribute to people needing healing across the entire world. Some pains are universal, and we should be a vessel to help others when the opportunity presents itself. Mental healthcare professionals have long discovered that like-minded people who want better in life find strength in being transparent and sharing. I am already sensing peace from writing this memoir, and the healing process has accelerated. I poured my all into each word and page. Sharing behind the scene moments of one's life is no easy task, regardless of your struggle or lack thereof. We all have a story. My anticipation boils over with each word I type. There is freedom in sharing, whether for happy times or joking about serious issues so that they can be digested and blended into life.

Although my brothers and I are able to joke about our abuse, the laughs stop when we think of my stepmother. Even while experiencing abuse, she found a way to help us as kids and forged a better life for us. My stepmom's intervening when my dad's anger riled him up blocked some physical torture, but she could not block the emotional damage inflicted by years of abuse and countless forceful blows. My dad did not know how to express himself. I know this to be true from what I witnessed during childhood until the present day.

Trying to stop my mother from getting abused and visualizations from the scene of her getting beaten by him in the Iberville Projects are permanently indented in my memory, along with the list of other nightmares I experienced while awake during my childhood. There is no human being who can erase that. There is always some cease to the fire in the midst of war, and my stepmom has been that for me.

Just like everyone who has experienced turmoil in their lives, I want closure. I am far from sure if my father conceptualized the way he treated me. I will not single out what he did to me as exclusive, but I am not in the heads of my siblings, mom, or stepmom.

Many other things had to happen to get me to where I am now. My near-death experience provoked a side of my dad I dreamed about and never knew existed. My father showed compassion for a son who felt unloved by the man he wanted to be loved by the most. Because of that, I remain hopeful about the future and feel that closure is coming soon.

Making adjustments to how I think and operate is a big step in maturing. I always wanted someone to look up to and deeply desired for that person to be my dad. However, he never left me much choice but to look elsewhere. Yes, he complimented my playing skills, but the emotional bond of a typical father and son never existed. I am still on the road to making adjustments for what has been missing in my life in this department. While the opportunity exists, I deeply desire to build a relationship with my father. Our history makes me intentional about relating to everyone I encounter in a positive manner. I purposely recall what I do not want and vow not to recreate or project that on anyone else. History does not have to repeat itself.

I am proud to say that I've put forth effort on my end. No, my dad and I do not talk very much, but I occasionally make an attempt at relationship redemption or closure for what happened in the past. After the last beat down, I was able to step out and feel what it was like to have some freedom as a teenager. Those were some of my best times, aside from football. One thing I am grateful for pertaining to my father is our mutual love for football. We connected effortlessly from day one on that matter.

My relationship with my dad is an oxymoron. I wonder if he thought that proudly bragging about me in public was supposed to compensate for the pain he caused me in private. Could my strong resemblance of my mother influence my father's maltreatment? Sometimes you have to take the conflict life presents and settle for any degree of positivity it may hold.

I couldn't imagine the burden and consequences my dad faced due to not having his father around. That is mental anguish and a substantial obstacle for any child. If you know your upbringing's dysfunction, you should have the conviction to do better when it is your turn. Unfortunately, that is not the way he thought. He called his shenanigans "tough love," and his attitude was "oh well!" He would not wrap his head around the fact that "oh well" did not work for him, and he had a chance to become more than the dad he never had.

The purpose of each generation should be to ensure the next one is in a better place. My dad surpassed his father's efforts, and his treatment assured me that I would relate to my son in an improved manner than what my siblings and I experienced. Closure comes in pieces, and I will work until the puzzle is complete.

Now that I've arrived at adulthood, I notice that I'm still on a mission to impress my dad. Back then, those efforts came on the football field, and subconsciously they still do. However, I want my dad to see how far I've come and how his actions affected me. His disclosure of his feelings caused me to pour out mine.

We have yet to communicate on anything substantial. I've accepted the fact that he may not know how to express what he feels. Hopefully, he can learn from my actions of functioning oppositely or find healing in another manner if I can't be the one to provide it.

By experience, I can vouch that the best relief will come when the truth is faced. Surviving abuse is never easy, especially when the mental anguish equals or outweighs the physical damage. Also, many abuse victims are subject to the abuser justifying their disrespect, which should never occur. I am proud to be a voice and an advocate for helping to prevent abuse of all forms.

I am confident that I still haven't reached my heights in football, but I am not ignorant of the fact that I can't play the game I love forever at a professional level. Being freed from the bondage of my pain propelled my search for other stress relieving methods aside from football. Opening up to you about my journey has served as a highlight in my healing process. I hope it helps heal any of your wounds that lie internally or on the surface. We often get so caught up in the mix that we lose sight of all the beautiful aspects life has to offer.

All the opportunities that life is offering me are drawing me closer to being far away from the memories that felt as strong as living and breathing football. Sharing my life story and fighting through the unthinkable to accomplish lifelong goals infuses me with the courage to walk boldly into the future with my head up and chest out. I do not handle the knowledge lightly that my life has been favored. I can vividly see that I am far from my past and closer to a dynamic future. There is always light at the end of the tunnel, and I've successfully made it out. Telling my truth is already proving to be a promising start.

Made in the USA
Middletown, DE
09 June 2023

31925740R00086